Pub Walks & Cycle Rides

The Lake District & Cumbria

Walk routes researched and written by Chris Bagshaw, Bill Birkett, Sheila Bowker, Paddy Dillon, John Gillham, Dennis Kelsall, Terry Marsh, Moira McCrossan, Jon Sparks, Hugh Taylor and David Winpenny
Cycle routes researched and written by Jon Sparks
Series managing editor: David Hancock

Produced by AA Publishing
© Automobile Association Developments Limited 2005
First published 2005

Published by AA Publishing (a trading name of Automobile Association Developments Limited, whose registered office is Southwood East, Apollo Rise, Farnborough, Hampshire, GU14 0JW; registered number 1878835).

A02013

Ordnance Survey® This product includes mapping data licensed from Ordnance Survey® with the permission of the Controller of Her Majesty's Stationery Office. ©Crown copyright 2005. All rights reserved. Licence number 399221.

ISBN-10: 0-7495-4452-X
ISBN-13: 978-0-7495-4452-2

A CIP catalogue record for this book is available from the British Library.

The contents of this book are believed correct at the time of printing. Nevertheless, the publishers cannot be held responsible for any errors or omissions or for changes in the details given in this book or for the consequences of any reliance on the information it provides. We have tried to ensure accuracy in this book, but things do change and we would be grateful if readers would advise us of any inaccuracies they may encounter. This does not affect your statutory rights.

We have taken all reasonable steps to ensure that these walks and cycle rides are safe and achievable by people with a realistic level of fitness. However, all outdoor activities involve a degree of risk and the publishers accept no responsibility for any injuries caused to readers whilst following these walks and cycle rides. For advice on walking and cycling in safety, see pages 12 to 15.

Visit AA Publishing's website www.theAA.com/bookshop

Page layouts by Pentacorbig, High Wycombe
Colour reproduction by Keene Group, Andover
Printed in Spain by Graficas Estella

AA

Pub Walks & Cycle Rides

The Lake District & Cumbria

Locator map

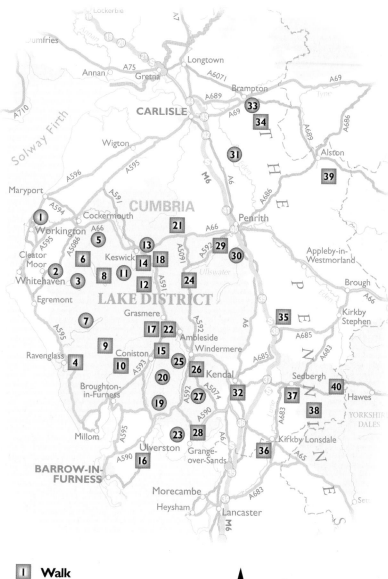

Contents

Picture on page 4: Ullswater beyond lush Gowbarrow Fell

Contents

The Lake District and Cumbria

This part of the country has long been a favourite with walkers and with families looking for a holiday offering beautiful scenery and outdoor activities. As the name suggests, it's full of lakes, which, paradoxically are not named 'lakes', but rather 'meres' or 'waters'. It is less well-known as a destination for cycling, but there's plenty of choice, with the Coast-to-Coast cycle route, a sculpture trail at Rowrah and trails in Grizedale Forest with the chance to see deer and even buzzards. Cycling in the Lake District just wouldn't be the same without following a route by water, so you can circle Ennerdale Water, start a route at England's deepest lake, Wast Water, or pedal by England's largest lake, Windermere.

weather is fine you can take a steam-yacht trip on Windermere, while a rainy-day option is a visit to Aquarium of the Lakes, on the southern tip of Windermere. The linear walk over Muncaster Fell has the added bonus of a return journey on a steam train on the Ravenglass and Eskdale Railway.

Your walk can have a literary theme as the area around the remote village of Seathwaite and Duddon Valley was a favourite with the poet, William Wordsworth, and the Lake district is well-known as Beatrix Potter country. The region has many historic sites which you pass on route, such as Castlerigg Stone Circle, and the tumuli and stone circle on Birkrigg Common. In Kendal, there are the remains of two castles, Kendal Castle and Castle Howe. Churches range from tiny St John's in the Vale on the walk from Legburthwaite, to the church at Cartmel Priory.

The landscape and peace and quiet are the reasons most people come to the region, so this book includes a route around tranquil Souther Fell and one through Winster Valley. Natural features you can see include the Wallowbarrow Gorge, Scafell Pike (England's highest peak) and Skelwith Force waterfall, which is passed on the walk from Elterwater. Waterside walks include the Lake District's least talked-about lake, Loweswater, as well as Derwent Water, Elterwater and Ullswater.

One other factor which may help you to decide which route to follow, is the nature of the pub we suggest. Indeed, the region is rich with unpretentious pubs, many of which are former coaching inns, housed in centuries-old buildings. The friendly Eagles Head pub on the Grizedale Forest ride says it all with its sign stating 'Walkers and cyclists are always welcome, however muddy'.

Routes take in some well-known places such as busy Keswick with its wide selection of places to eat and drink, Ambleside with its profusion of outdoor-gear shops, the tourist destination of Bowness-on-Windermere and the seaside resort of Grange-over-Sands. Famous Buttermere offers a lake, a valley and a village. Places to visit before or after your walk or ride include the Beatrix Potter Gallery in Hawkshead and the Lakeland Motor Museum at Holker Hall by Cark. If the

The beautiful view from the shores of Loweswater

Using this book

Each walk and cycle ride has a coloured panel giving essential information for the walker and cyclist, including the distance, terrain, nature of the paths, and where to park your car.

1 MINIMUM TIME: The time stated for completing each route is the estimated minimum time that a reasonably fit family group of walkers or cyclists would take to complete the circuit. This does not allow for rest or refreshment stops.

2 MAPS: Each route is shown on a detailed map. However, some detail is lost because of the restrictions imposed by scale, so for this reason, we recommend that you use the maps in conjunction with a more detailed Ordnance Survey map. The relevant Ordnance Survey Explorer map appropriate for each walk or cycle is listed.

3 START/FINISH: Here we indicate the start location and parking area. There is a six-figure grid reference prefixed by two letters showing which 100km square of the National Grid it refers to. You'll find more information on grid references on most Ordnance Survey maps.

4 LEVEL OF DIFFICULTY: The walks and cycle rides have been graded simply (1 to 3) to give an indication of their relative difficulty. Easier routes, such as those with little total ascent, on easy footpaths or level trails, or those covering shorter distances are graded 1. The hardest routes, either

---

1 **3h00** **8.5 MILES** **13.7 KM** **LEVEL 1**23 **4**

SHORTER ALTERNATIVE ROUTE

1h30 **4 MILES** **6.4 KM** **LEVEL 1**23

2 ─ **MAP:** OS Explorer OL24 White Peak

3 **START/FINISH:** Rudyard Old Station, grid ref SJ 955579

TRAILS/TRACKS: old railway trackbed

LANDSCAPE: wooded lake shore, peaceful pastures and meadows

PUBLIC TOILETS: Rudyard village

5 ─ **TOURIST INFORMATION:** Leek, tel 01538 483741

6 ─ **CYCLE HIRE:** none near by

THE PUB: The Abbey Inn, Leek, see Directions to the pub, page 27

7 ─ ❶ Take care along the banks of the lake – keep well away from the shore line

---

because they include a lot of ascent, greater distances, or are in hilly, more demanding terrains, are graded 3.

5 TOURIST INFORMATION: The nearest tourist information office and contact number is given for further local information, in particular opening details for the attractions listed in the 'Where to go from here' section.

6 CYCLE HIRE: We list, within reason, the nearest cycle hire shop/centre.

7 ❶ Here we highlight any potential difficulties or dangers along the route. At a glance you will know if the walk is steep or crosses difficult terrain, or if a cycle route is hilly, encounters a main road, or whether a mountain bike is essential for the off-road trails. If a particular route is suitable for older, fitter children we say so here.

About the pub

Generally, all the pubs featured are on the walk or cycle route. Some are close to the start/finish point, others are at the midway point, and occasionally, the recommended pub is a short drive from the start/finish point. We have included a cross-section of pubs, from homely village locals and isolated rural gems to traditional inns and upmarket country pubs which specialise in food. What they all have in common is that they serve food and welcome children.

The description of the pub is intended to convey its history and character and in the 'food' section we list a selection of dishes, which indicate the style of food available. Under 'family facilities', we say if the pub offers a children's menu or smaller portions of adult dishes, and whether the pub has a family room, highchairs, baby-changing facilities, or toys. There is detail on the garden, terrace, and any play area.

DIRECTIONS: If the pub is very close to the start point we state see Getting to the Start. If the pub is on the route the relevant direction/map location number is given, in addition to general directions. In some cases the pub is a short drive away from the finish point, so we give detailed directions to the pub from the end of the route.

PARKING: The number of parking spaces is given. All but a few of the walks and rides start away from the pub. If the pub car park is the parking/start point, then we have been given permission by the landlord to print the fact. You should always let the landlord or a member of staff know that you are using the car park before setting off.

OPEN: If the pub is open all week we state 'daily' and if it's open throughout the day we say 'all day', otherwise we just give the days/sessions the pub is closed.

FOOD: If the pub serves food all week we state 'daily' and if food is served throughout the day we say 'all day', otherwise we just give the days/sessions when food is not served.

BREWERY/COMPANY: This is the name of the brewery to which the pub is tied or the pub company that owns it. 'Free house' means that the pub is independently owned and run.

REAL ALE: We list the regular real ales available on handpump. 'Guest beers' indicates that the pub rotates beers from a number of microbreweries.

DOGS: We say if dogs are allowed in pubs on walk routes and detail any restrictions.

ROOMS: We list the number of bedrooms and how many are en suite. For prices please call the pub.

Please note that pubs change hands frequently and new chefs are employed, so menu details and facilities may change at short notice. Not all the pubs featured in this guide are listed in the *AA Pub Guide*. For information on those that are, including AA-rated accommodation, and for a comprehensive selection of pubs across Britain, please refer to the *AA Pub Guide* or see the AA's website www.theAA.com

Alternative refreshment stops

Most routes have information about other pubs or cafés along the way. If there are no other places on the route, we list the nearest village or town where you can find somewhere else to eat and drink.

☛ Where to go from here

Many of the routes are short and may only take a few hours. You may wish to explore the surrounding area after lunch or before tackling the route, so we have selected a few attractions with children in mind.

Walking and cycling in safety

WALKING

All the walks are suitable for families, but less experienced family groups, especially those with younger children, should try the shorter or easier walks first. Route finding is usually straightforward, but the maps are for guidance only and we recommend that you always take the suggested Ordnance Survey map with you.

Risks

Although each walk has been researched with a view to minimising any risks, no walk in the countryside can be considered to be completely free from risk. Walking in the outdoors will always require a degree of common sense and judgement to ensure that it is as safe as possible, especially for young children.

- Be particularly careful on cliff paths and in upland terrain, where the consequences of a slip can be serious.
- Remember to check tidal conditions before walking on the seashore.
- Some sections of route are by, or cross, busy roads. Remember traffic is a danger even on minor country lanes.
- Be careful around farmyard machinery and livestock.
- Be aware of the consequences of changes in the weather and check the forecast before you set out. Ensure the whole family is properly equipped, wearing warm clothing and a good pair of boots or sturdy walking shoes. Take waterproof clothing with you and carry spare clothing and a torch if you are walking in the winter months. Remember the weather can change quickly at any time of the year, and in moorland and heathland areas, mist and fog can make route finding much harder. In summer, take account of the heat and sun by wearing a hat and carrying enough water.

- On walks away from centres of population you should carry a whistle and survival bag. If you do have an accident requiring emergency services, make a note of your position as accurately as possible and dial 999.

CYCLING

Cycling is a fun activity which children love, and teaching your child to ride a bike, and going on family cycling trips, are rewarding experiences. Not only is cycling a great way to travel, but as a regular form of exercise it can make an invaluable contribution to a child's health and fitness, and increase their confidence and sense of independence.

The growth of motor traffic has made Britain's roads increasingly dangerous and unattractive to cyclists. Cycling with children is an added responsibility and, as with everything, there is a risk when taking them out for a day's cycling. However, in recent years many measures have been taken to address this, including the on-going development of the National Cycle Network (8,000 miles utilising quiet lanes and traffic-free paths) and local designated off-road routes for families, such as converted railway lines, canal tow paths and forest tracks.

In devising the cycle rides in this guide, every effort has been made to use these designated cycle paths, or to link them with quiet country lanes and waymarked byways and bridleways. Unavoidably, in a few cases, some relatively busy B-roads have been used to link the quieter, more attractive routes.

Rules of the road

- Ride in single file on narrow and busy roads.
- Be alert, look and listen for traffic, especially on narrow lanes and blind bends and be extra careful when descending steep hills, as loose gravel can lead to an accident.
- In wet weather make sure you keep a good distance between you and other riders.
- Make sure you indicate your intentions clearly.
- Brush up on *The Highway Code* before venturing out on to the road.

Off-road safety code of conduct

- Only ride where you know it is legal to do so. It is forbidden to cycle on public footpaths, marked in yellow. The only 'rights of way' open to cyclists are bridleways (blue markers) and unsurfaced tracks, known as byways, which are open to all traffic and waymarked in red.
  - Canal tow paths: you need a permit to cycle on some stretches of tow path (www.waterscape.com). Remember that access paths can be steep and slippery and always get off and push your bike under low bridges and by locks.

- Always yield to walkers and horses, giving adequate warning of your approach.
- Don't expect to cycle at high speeds.
- Keep to the main trail to avoid any unnecessary erosion to the area beside the trail and to prevent skidding, especially if it is wet.
- Remember the Country Code.

Cycling with children

Children can use a child seat from the age of eight months, or from the time they can hold themselves upright. There are a number of child seats available which fit on the front or rear of a bike and towable two-seat trailers are worth investigating. 'Trailer bicycles', suitable for five- to ten-year-olds, can be attached to the rear of an adult's bike, so that the adult has control, allowing the child to pedal if he/she wishes. Family cycling can be made easier by using a tandem, as it can carry a child seat and tow trailers. 'Kiddy-cranks' for shorter legs can be fitted to the rear seat tube, enabling either parent to take their child out cycling. With older children it is better to purchase the right size bike rather than one that is too big, as an oversized bike will be difficult to control, and so potentially dangerous.

Preparing your bicycle

A basic routine includes checking the wheels for broken spokes or excess play in the bearings, and checking the tyres for punctures, undue wear and the correct tyre pressures. Ensure that the brake blocks are firmly in place and not worn, and that cables are not frayed or too slack. Lubricate hubs, pedals, gear mechanisms and cables. Make sure you have a pump, a bell, a rear rack to carry panniers and, if cycling at night, a set of working lights.

Preparing yourself

Equipping the family with cycling clothing need not be an expensive exercise. Comfort is the key when considering what to wear. Essential items for well-being on a bike are

padded cycling shorts, warm stretch leggings (avoid tight-fitting and seamed trousers like jeans or baggy tracksuit trousers that may become caught in the chain), stiff-soled training shoes, and a wind and waterproof jacket. Fingerless gloves will add to your comfort.

A cycling helmet provides essential protection if you fall off your bike, so they are particularly recommended for young children learning to cycle.

Wrap your child up with several layers in colder weather. Make sure you and those with you are easily visible by car drivers and other road users, by wearing light-coloured or luminous clothing in daylight and reflective strips or sashes in failing light and when it is dark.

What to take with you

Invest in a pair of medium-sized panniers (rucksacks are unwieldy and can affect balance) to carry the necessary gear for you and your family for the day. Take extra clothes with you, the amount depending on the season, and always pack a light wind/waterproof jacket. Carry a basic tool kit (tyre levers, adjustable spanner, a small screwdriver, puncture repair kit, a set of Allen keys) and practical spares, such as an inner tube, a universal brake/gear cable, and a selection of nuts and bolts. Also, always take a pump and a strong lock.

Cycling, especially in hilly terrain and off-road, saps energy, so take enough food and drink for your outing. Always carry plenty of water, especially in hot and humid weather conditions. Consume high-energy snacks like cereal bars, cake or fruits, eating little and often to combat feeling weak and tired. Remember that children get thirsty (and hungry) much more quickly than adults so always have food and diluted juices available for them.

Finally, the most important advice of all is enjoy yourselves!

USEFUL CYCLING WEBSITES

NATIONAL CYCLE NETWORK
A comprehensive network of safe and attractive cycle routes throughout the UK.
It is co-ordinated by the route construction charity Sustrans with the support of more than 450 local authorities and partners across Britain. For maps, leaflets and more information on the designated off-road cycle trails across the country contact
www.sustrans.org.uk
www.nationalcyclenetwork.org.uk

LONDON CYCLING CAMPAIGN
Pressure group that lobbies MPs, organises campaigns and petitions in order to improve cycling conditions in the capital. It provides maps, leaflets and information on cycle routes across London.
www.lcc.org.uk

BRITISH WATERWAYS
For information on towpath cycling, visit
www.waterscape.com

FORESTRY COMMISSION
For information on cycling in Forestry Commission woodland see
www.forestry.gov.uk/recreation

CYCLISTS TOURING CLUB
The largest cycling club in Britain, provides information on cycle touring, and legal and technical matters
www.ctc.org.uk

Sea views from the Seaton Track

An easy ride along a former railway with views to coast and fells.

Coast-to-coast route

Several other routes in this book share sections of the C2C (Coast-to-Coast) cycle route, but this one overlooks the start, at the end of a promontory which can be seen beyond Workington harbour. It's traditional for riders to dip their feet (or their wheels) in the sea at each end – this is easier when the tide is in! There's an alternative start to the C2C in Whitehaven, and the two branches meet near Keswick. There are also alternative finishes on the east coast, either at Tynemouth or Sunderland. The full route is around 140 miles (225km) and the record time is under nine hours, though most people take three or four days and some make a much more leisurely passage.

The Roman remains at Burrow Walls were part of a fort that formed a line of sea defences, possibly extending as far south as Ravenglass. This is sometimes considered to be an extension of Hadrian's Wall. Nearby Siddick Pond, a nature reserve, is an important area of wetland habitat consisting of meres and reed beds. It is very close to a large paper mill, which has managed to clean up its emissions substantially in recent years, encouraging wildlife to flourish.

the ride

1 From the parking area outside the **post office** follow a surfaced path left and up to the level of the old railway. Continue, away from the bridges. As you pass under a bridge on the outskirts of Seaton, the views begin to open up. The landscape still has its industrial element, but there is also the Irish Sea and Solway Firth, with the Galloway hills beyond on a clear day. As the route begins to curve to the left under another bridge, you'll glimpse the rooftops of **Workington**. Just beyond this, some rough walls in the field on the left are the remains of **Burrow Walls** Roman fort.

Top: Roman remains at Burrow Walls, Seaton
Left: Bridge at Seaton, with decorated barriers

| 1h00 | 6.75 MILES | 10.9 KM | LEVEL 1 2 3 |

MAP: OS Explorer 303 Whitehaven and Workington
START/FINISH: Seaton town centre; grid ref: NY 017307
TRAILS/TRACKS: old railway track with tarmac surface; optional return on minor lanes with some grass and stony tracks
LANDSCAPE: farmland with sea and fell views, some industrial landscape
PUBLIC TOILETS: none on route
TOURIST INFORMATION: Workington, tel 01900 606699
CYCLE HIRE: Keswick Mountain Bikes, Keswick, tel 017687 75202
THE PUB: The Coachman Inn, Seaton, near start of route

❶ The railway path is suitable for children of all ages. On the return road loop there are two steep climbs and one steep descent, suitable for more experienced family groups; children 10+

On the right is **Siddick Pond**, with wind turbines beyond. You soon reach a track junction with a **C2C sign.**

2 Branch down to the right for a closer look at Siddick Pond, then return to the junction and keep straight on. The route winds through a broad cutting then runs out onto a green-railed bridge over the **A596** on the outskirts of Workington. At the further end of the bridge is the **Hagworm Wiggle Path**.

3 For an easy and entirely off-road path, turn round here and retrace the route to **Seaton**. To extend this shorter ride, continue over the bridge and along the railway track for another 2 miles (3.2km) to Point 5. For the alternative, more challenging return loop from Point 3, roll down towards the bridge over the **River Derwent**. Just before reaching it bear left. Cross a grassy area and follow an emerging track bearing left into a new **underpass** below the main road. This leads out to a lane.

Getting to the start
Seaton is a village 2 miles (3.2km) north of Workington. Approaching from Workington, the main road swings left then dips towards a railway bridge decorated with cycling figures. Turn left before the bridge, at a sign 'Library'. Park in the spaces on the right, outside the post office, or on the street.

Why do this cycle ride?
There's plenty to engage the interest on this simple ride along a well-surfaced old railway, be it fine views over the sea in one direction and the Lakeland Fells in the other, or the remains of the Roman fort at Burrow Walls and a rich variety of wayside flowers.

Researched and written by: Jon Sparks

4 Continue in the same general direction, initially running parallel to the river. Continue along the narrow surfaced lane, ignoring various gravel tracks branching off. After a **row of cottages** the lane becomes rougher. Keep right at a fork, down to the river.

5 Turn left (upstream). Bump through the cobbled yard at **Seaton Mill** then swing left over a small bridge and bear right at a **Cumbria Cycleway sign**. A stiff climb leads to a T-junction on the outskirts of Seaton. Turn right, back on tarmac. Emerge onto a junction with a grassy island, in front of the **Packhorse pub** and turn right. Follow the lane, climbing gently, with fine views of the Lakeland Fells. The lane levels off and then dips slightly at a gravel lay-by. The railway track is close by on the left and runs parallel for the next 0.5 mile (800m), but save this for the return as the lane gives better views.

The lane begins to descend – take care as the descent becomes steep and twisting as it drops into **Camerton** village. Keep left past the **Black Lion pub** and quickly down through the gears as the road climbs steeply out of the village, peaking as it reaches a railway bridge.

6 Immediately before the bridge there's a **cycleway sign** on the left. Negotiate the wiggle barrier and follow the narrow path as it drops down to the railway track at a short section of 'dual carriageway'. The left branch keeps the views for a few yards but they soon rejoin. Continue level and then gently downhill, through a tree-lined cutting and then under a bridge with another wrought-iron wiggle. Pass some railings, then cross the bridges in the centre of **Seaton**. Make a sharp left turn to drop back down the path to the **post office car park**.

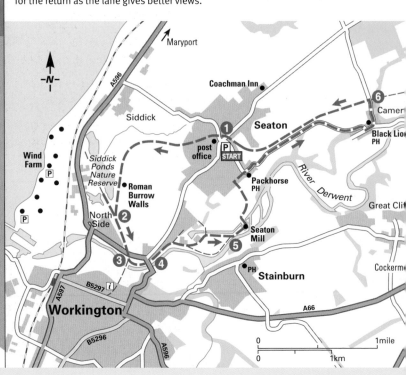

The Coachman Inn

about the pub

The Coachman Inn
43 High Seaton, Seaton
Workington, Cumbria CA14 1LJ
Tel 01900 603976

DIRECTIONS:	on the north eastern edge of Seaton
PARKING:	30
OPEN:	closed Tuesday
FOOD:	daily
BREWERY/COMPANY:	Scottish & Newcastle
REAL ALE:	none available

It isn't recommended to cycle the 0.5 mile (800m) to The Coachman if you have younger children in tow. The road is relatively busy and it's uphill all the way. Whether you arrive on two wheels or four, the pub is friendly, unpretentious, and well used to cyclists, being close to both the Coast-to-Coast route and the Cumbria Cycleway. Hearty appetites are therefore well catered for with an extensive and reasonably priced menu that includes all the usual pub favourites and a good number of vegetarian options. The beer garden is tucked away at the rear, well away from the road, though this means it doesn't get the views that the pub's elevated position promises.

Food

Main menu dishes include home-made steak pie, lasagne, farmhouse grill, scampi and chips and vegetarian dishes such as Stilton and vegetable crumble. Look to the specials board for hot and cold baguettes – Cumberland sausage and fried onions. Separate sandwich menu.

Family facilities

The Coachman is a friendly family pub offering a warm welcome to children, a children's menu and a good beer garden.

Alternative refreshment stops

Pubs and cafés in Seaton town centre; on the route you'll find the Packhorse at Low Seaton and the Black Lion in Camerton.

☛ Where to go from here

Maryport's Maritime Museum tells the story of the town's maritime tradition (www.lakedistrict-coastaquarium. co.uk). Alternatively, pay a visit to The Senhouse Roman Museum which contains an impressive collection of Roman artefacts dug from the former fort next door.

A sculpture trail from Rowrah

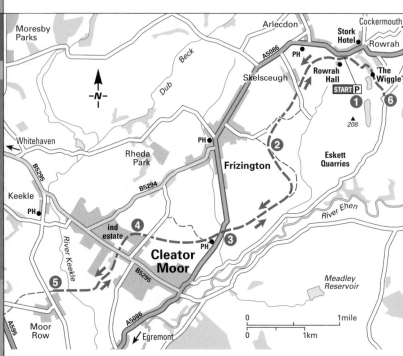

An easy linear ride along
a sculpture trail, rich in
industrial heritage.

Sculptures and wild flowers

The sculptures scattered along this route
are a source of constant interest, with a
personal favourite in the great crown-like
arrangement of iron and timber on the
elevated section. Get more information
on all the sculptures from the Sustrans
website, www.sustrans.org.uk: click on
'Interactive Mapping'.

Near the final turn (Point 6), you'll
see a sign for High Leas nature reserve.
It consists of five pristine wildflower

meadows – now a very rare sight – and a
fragment of an ancient agricultural system.
They are home to several species of orchid,
and the two lower fields also have lady's
mantle and adder's-tongue. It's interesting
to contrast these flower-rich fields with
those on the other side of the track.

The cutting below Frizington is one of
the most interesting sections of the route.
The banks on the east side, which are
relatively sunny, are covered in flowers
through spring and summer. Notable are the
fluffy purple-blue heads of scabious, much
loved by butterflies such as the red admiral.

*A bicycle propped against a National Cycle
Network sign at Rowrah*

Also present are vivid blue speedwell and wild strawberry. The opposite wall, which is much shadier and consequently damper, supports masses of ferns. A common species, with delicate dark green fronds, is maidenhair spleenwort, and the nearby station platform is overrun with it.

The cave in this cutting is not specially salubrious, but worth a quick look. The reddish colour and 'soapy' texture of the rock indicate the presence of haematite, the main ore mineral for the iron industry. This cave would have been a trial dig to see if the iron concentration improved.

the ride

1 Turn right out of the car park and back up the bumpy track, then keep straight on past the bridge and down a surfaced track on to the **railway line** proper. Follow

1h30 — 11.5 MILES — 18.5 KM — LEVEL 1 2 3

MAP: OS Explorer OL 4 The English Lakes (NW) or OS Explorer 303 Whitehaven and Workington

START/FINISH: car park at Rowrah; grid ref: NY 056185

TRAILS/TRACKS: almost entirely on good gritty tracks

LANDSCAPE: rolling farmland and woodland, views to fells

PUBLIC TOILETS: none on route

TOURIST INFORMATION: Whitehaven, tel 01946 852939

CYCLE HIRE: Ainfield Cycle Centre, Cleator, tel 01946 812427; Mark Taylor Cycles, Whitehaven, tel 01946 692252

THE PUB: Stork Hotel, Rowrah, near start of route

🔴 Suitability: any age

Getting to the start

Rowrah is 9 miles (14.5km) south of Cockermouth on the A5086. On a slight bend at the south end of the village (just before the sign for Arlecdon) is a track off to the left, signposted to Rowrah Hall and 'Cycleway car park'. Follow this over a bridge then turn left on a rough track. Take care here as this is part of the cycle route. In 150yds (137m) there is an open space on the left; park here.

Why do this cycle ride?

This ride is so packed with interest that its out-and-back nature is a positive advantage. It allows you two chances to enjoy the wayside flowers, two chances to admire the views in the middle section, and a second chance to see if you missed any sculptures the first time around.

Researched and written by: Jon Sparks

this past the old station platforms below **Skelsceugh**, and about 1 mile (1.6km) further on reach a junction.

2 Bear right over a little **bridge** (the other branch doubles back under this and up to Frizington). A direction marker points you to Cleator Moor, Moor Row and Whitehaven. Continue along the trackbed, past more crumbling platforms, and then into a shady tree-lined cutting. There's exposed limestone rock in places and a small cave. Emerge onto a contrasting elevated section, with more expansive views, especially left towards the valley of **Ennerdale** and its surrounding fells. Go through another wooded section and cross an iron-railed bridge over the **A5086**.

3 Just after this a large **boulder** beside the track shows all the signs of having been shaped by ice – look for the striations (gouges) made by rocks embedded in the base of the glacier. A track then crosses the route: it takes some skill to negotiate the barriers here without putting a foot down. Continue along a stretch where the trees meet overhead, and keep ahead until the surfaced track runs out.

4 Bear half left (signed for Cleator Moor, Moor Row and Whitehaven), continue past an **industrial estate**, and under a road with finely decorated bridge arches. Keep straight on, signed to Moor Row and Whitehaven, following the main line of the track, guided by more signs for **Whitehaven**, until you reach another old station platform, with some interesting **sculptures**. Beyond this the surroundings become more urban, so it's a good turnaround point. (However, you can continue all the way into Whitehaven if you wish.)

5 On the return see if you missed any sculptures. Some are quite unassuming, like the seat built into one of the old platforms, or the squirrels and owls on top of wooden fence posts on the outskirts of Cleator Moor.

When you get back to the **car park** it's well worth continuing on the track, forking right past a barrier. Follow the track through a cutting with some exposed rock, then loop round left to avoid some old quarry workings (these are partly flooded – heed the warning signs). This takes you through 'The Wiggle', a sculpture of curved stone walls by Robert Drake. Cross a small **bridge** and in the woods beyond, watch out for red squirrels. Pass another sculpture – two pieces of rock taken from the same block. Beyond this the path may be muddy in winter. A **National Cycle Network sign** tells you that it's 21 miles (33.8km) to Keswick and 120 miles (193km) to Sunderland, and the route rises to meet a lane. Go up the rise to see if you can work out the puzzle of the pedestrian gate alongside the small cattle grid for bikes – the instructions are all in symbols.

6 Turn around here to return to the **car park**.

A wayside sculpture with Crag Fell in the distance

Stork Hotel

The Stork is only five minutes' walk from the cycleway car park (we say 'walk' advisedly, because the busy road is not comfortable for family cycling). It's not a place that gives itself airs, but it does offer comfortable surroundings, a warm welcome, locally brewed Jennings beer and a wide range of reasonably priced pub food in generous portions. Though you might need to have cycled a little

about the pub

Stork Hotel
Rowrah Road, Rowrah
Frizington, Cumbria CA26 3XJ
Tel 01946 861213

DIRECTIONS: on the main road through the village

PARKING: 6

OPEN: daily, and all day Saturday and Sunday

FOOD: daily

BREWERY/COMPANY: free house

REAL ALE: Black Sheep Bitter, Jennings Cumberland Ale

ROOMS: 6 bedrooms

further before you feel entitled to a Stork 'Big Grill', which includes Sirloin steak, lamb chop, bacon chop, Cumberland sausage, black pudding and all the trimmings. There's a limited amount of outside seating, which is close to the road but does have super views to the fells.

Food
If you don't fancy the mammoth mixed grill, try the suet crust steak pie, salmon with white wine and dill sauce, or the freshly battered cod and chips. Ploughman's lunches and salads are also served.

Family facilities
The Stork is ideal for families. There are highchairs available for younger children and a 'grubs up' menu for smaller appetites – bangers and mash, burgers, pasta bolognaise. Small portions of meals on the main menu are also available.

Alternative refreshment stops
There is a pub at Parkside (on the A5086, Point 3) close to the halfway point; also pubs just off the route at Frizington and Cleator Moor.

☛ Where to go from here
See 19 different breeds of sheep at the Lakeland Sheep and Wool Centre, Cockermouth, plus sheepdog demonstrations in summer (www.sheep-woolcentre.co.uk).

Wild Ennerdale

A ride through the forest beyond Ennerdale Water.

Ennerdale

Pillar Rock, south east of the lake end, stands proud of the mountainside in a way that few other crags do, and has a distinct summit of its own. This was first reached in 1826 by a local shepherd, John Atkinson. If conditions are good there may well be climbers on the Rock – binoculars will help you spot them. Today the easiest routes to the top are considered as hard scrambling rather than rock-climbing, but over the years climbers have added many routes on the various faces, some of them very challenging.

Some forty years ago the legendary fellwalker Alfred Wainwright wrote, 'Afforestation in Ennerdale has cloaked the lower slopes…in a dark and funereal shroud of foreign trees'. But things are changing. The Forestry Commission now plants a wider diversity of trees in many of its forests, and in the upper reaches of Ennerdale things have gone much further.

The Wild Ennerdale project is slowly restoring much more natural woodland. It's worth reflecting that the bare slopes of rough grass are not entirely 'natural' either, but the result of centuries of farming, most notably overgrazing by sheep.

the ride

1 Turn left from the **car park**, rolling down to the shores of **Ennerdale Water**. The track runs beside the lake for about 1 mile (1.6km), then continues through the forest above the river, here called **Char Dub**. Dub is a common dialect word for a pool, and the char is a species of fish. Continue past **Low Gillerthwaite Field Centre** and then the youth hostel at **High Gillerthwaite**.

2 Just past the youth hostel the track forks. Keep right (really straight ahead). The track goes up and down more than you might expect. Take care on fast downhill bends where the surface is loose. Above all don't grab at the brakes. At the next fork 1 mile (1.6km) further on, a sign to the right

2h00	12 MILES	19.3 KM	LEVEL 2

MAP: OS Explorer OL 4 The English Lakes (NW)

START/FINISH: Bowness Knott car park; grid ref: NY 109153

TRAILS/TRACKS: good forest roads, occasionally bumpy

LANDSCAPE: lake, forest, wild valley ringed by high fells

PUBLIC TOILETS: none on route

TOURIST INFORMATION: Egremont, tel 01946 820693

CYCLE HIRE: Ainfield Cycle Centre, Cleator, tel 01946 812427; Mark Taylor Cycles, Whitehaven, tel 01946 692252

THE PUB: Shepherds Arms Hotel, Ennerdale Bridge, near the route

🚫 Rough track on the last short section (400yds/366m) to Black Sail Hut – mountain bike and some skill required, or walk. Suitability: children 10+. Younger children will enjoy a shorter version

Getting to the start
The car park is half way along the north shore of Ennerdale Water, at a dead-end. Access is via minor roads east from Ennerdale Bridge or south from Lamplugh.

Why do this cycle ride?
Although relatively gentle in itself, this route joins the world of the mountaineer, the fell-runner and the long-distance walker, entering the heart of the high fells. At the head of the valley, lonely Black Sail Hut Youth Hostel makes a perfect place to stop. You can make yourself a cup of tea there and even stay the night – but make sure that you book in advance (tel 0411 108450, not open all year).

Researched and written by: Jon Sparks

points to Pillar. Save the Pillar road for the return and keep straight on – in fact, this track straight ahead gives the best views of the **Pillar Rock**. The way climbs gradually to a more level stretch with open views across the valley to Pillar directly opposite. Pillar Rock is the centrepiece of a mass of crags strewn across the north face of the mountain. This is a worthy objective in itself and makes a reasonable turnaround point for those who feel they've gone far enough.

3 As Pillar falls behind, the valley head opens up. There's a space where you may find some vehicles and then the main track curves down right.

4 Straight ahead through a gate is a much rougher track leading 400yds (366m) to **Black Sail Hut Youth Hostel** – many people may prefer to walk for some or all of it. You can make yourselves tea or coffee in the members' kitchen, but don't forget to leave a suitable donation. Return to the gate. The bridleway going up right climbs to Scarth Gap Pass and then descends to Buttermere. Ignore it, and go back through the gate and down left to the **River Liza**.

5 Splash through the concrete ford and swing round right. Now keep straight along the track, mostly downhill, ignoring branches up and left until it swings down to the **river**.

6 Cross the bridge and go up to the 'Pillar' signpost. Rejoin the main track of the outward route to return to the **car park**.

Top: Walkers beside Ennerdale Water
Left: Flowers on a rocky niche above Ennerdale Water

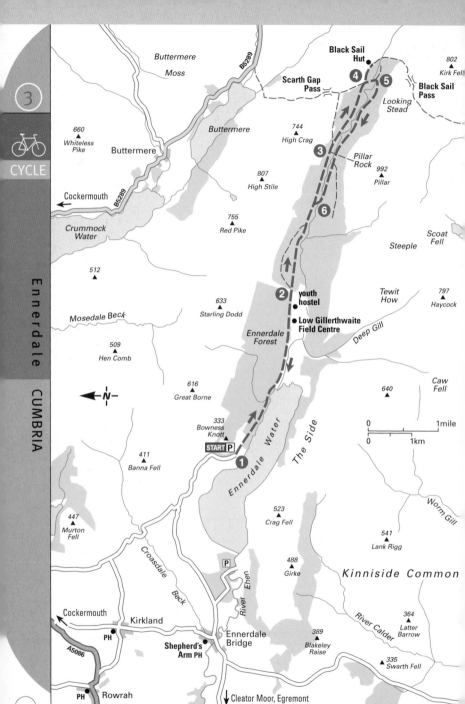

Ennerdale CUMBRIA

Buttermere
Moss

B5289

Black Sail
Hut

Scarth Gap
Pass

④ ⑤

Black Sail
Pass

802
▲
Kirk Fell

Looking
Stead

660
▲
Whiteless
Pike

Buttermere

Buttermere

744
▲
High Crag

③

Pillar
Rock

992
▲
Pillar

Cockermouth

B5289

807
▲
High Stile

⑥

Crummock
Water

755
▲
Red Pike

Scoat
Fell

Steeple

512
▲

Tewit
How

797
▲
Haycock

Mosedale Beck

633
▲
Starling Dodd

②   youth
     hostel

● Low Gillerthwaite
  Field Centre

Deep Gill

509
▲
Hen Comb

Ennerdale
Forest

–N–

616
▲
Great Borne

Caw
Fell

640
▲

333
Bowness
Knott

START P

①

0 ─────────── 1mile
0 ─────────── 1km

Ennerdale Water

The Side

Worm Gill

411
▲
Banna Fell

523
▲
Crag Fell

541
▲
Lank Rigg

447
▲
Murton
Fell

Croasdale Beck

P

488
▲
Girke

Kinniside Common

River Ehen

Cockermouth

A5086

Kirkland

PH

Shepherd's
Arm PH

Ennerdale
Bridge

389
▲
Blakeley
Raise

River Calder

364
▲
Latter
Barrow

335
▲
Swarth Fell

PH   Rowrah

↓ Cleator Moor, Egremont

Shepherds Arms Hotel

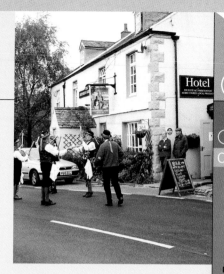

The Shepherds Arms Hotel sits at the heart of the village of Ennerdale Bridge, smack on the Coast-to-Coast walk. This cream-washed country inn is welcoming and homely, its traditionally furnished bar (wood floors, bookcases, open log fires) dispense cracking real ales and hearty, home-cooked food to refuel the weariest of cyclists. In fact, walkers and cyclists are important here, evidenced by the maps posted in the bar, and the weather forecast chalked up daily on a blackboard. In addition, the en suite bedrooms are very comfortable, with period furnishings and pleasant views, and a restful night's sleep is guaranteed.

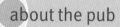

about the pub

Shepherds Arms Hotel
Ennerdale Bridge
Cumbria CA23 3AR
Tel 01946 861249
www.shepherdsarmshotel.co.uk

DIRECTIONS: in the centre of the village, 3.5 miles (5.7km) west of the start of the ride
PARKING: 6 (good street parking)
OPEN: daily, all day
FOOD: daily
BREWERY/COMPANY: free house
REAL ALE: Timothy Taylor Landlord, Coniston Bluebird, Jennings Bitter, guest beers
ROOMS: 8 bedrooms (6 en suite)

Food
From the bar menu, tuck into spinach and Wensleydale tart, local lamb chops, steak and ale pie with a suet crust, served with hand-cut chips or opt for something lighter like a warming bowl of soup, freshly made sandwiches and decent salads. Separate restaurant menu.

Family facilities
Children are welcome in the bars and overnight, with plenty of games and toys to keep them amused. There's a delightful garden, although it does border a fast-flowing stream, so supervision is necessary.

Alternative refreshment stops
None on route, although those venturing to Black Sail Youth Hostel (Point 4) can make themselves tea and coffee in the member's kitchen (donations).

☛ Where to go from here
The ruined 12th-century Egremont Castle is well worth a visit for its impressive red sandstone gatehouse. At the Florence Mine Heritage Centre just off the A595 you can tour the pit and see reconstructions of 19th-century pit life in the visitor centre.

Over Muncaster Fell

A walk from Ravenglass to Eskdale Green, returning on La'al Ratty.

Ravenglass and Eskdale

Muncaster Fell is a long and knobbly fell of no great height. The summit rises to 758ft (231m), but is a little off the route described. A winding path negotiates the fell from end to end and this can be linked with other paths and tracks to offer a fine walk from Ravenglass to Eskdale Green. It's a linear walk, but when the Ravenglass and Eskdale Railway is in full steam, a ride back on the train is simply a joy.

Affectionately known as La'al Ratty, the Ravenglass and Eskdale Railway has a history of fits and starts. It was originally opened as a standard gauge track in 1875 to serve a granite quarry, and was converted to narrow gauge between 1915 and 1917. After a period of closure it was bought by enthusiasts in 1960, overhauled and reopened, and is now a firm favourite. The line runs from Ravenglass to Dalegarth Station, near Boot at the head of Eskdale. The railway runs almost all year, but there are times in the winter when there are no services. Obtain a timetable and study it carefully. When the trains are running, there are few Lakeland journeys to compare with a trip both ways.

The Romans operated an important port facility at Ravenglass. Fortifications were built all the way around the Cumbrian coast to link with Hadrian's Wall and a Roman road cut through Eskdale, over the passes to Ambleside, then along the crest of High Street to link with the road network near Penrith.

A narrow-gauge train pulls into Ravenglass station on the Ravenglass and Eskdale Railway

the walk

1 Cross footbridges over the mainline and miniature railway lines, and continue along a narrow path. Turn right along a tree-lined lane signed to **Walls Castle**. A footpath/cycle track runs parallel on the left. The **bathhouse** is about 500yds (457m) along.

2 Continue along the footpath/cycle track, which swings left (signposted 'Muncaster') away from the tarmac road. Follow the track to an open view of **dunes** and the sea. Continue up a short way, then turn left before some **buildings**. Follow the track up a little wooded valley and past a small lake, then across fields and into another wood. Keep straight ahead (signed **Esk TR**) to an octagonal wooden building – the visitors' entrance to **Muncaster Castle** grounds. Turn left, under an arched gateway, to the main road.

3 Turn right. Cross the road beyond the **Muncaster Guest House**. The road leads up to a bend, where **Fell Lane** is signposted straight uphill. Climb steadily for 0.75 mile (1.2km). Reach a little wooded dip, fork right, then left, passing secluded **Muncaster Tarn** on the left. Go through a gate at the top of the track to open fellside.

what to look for

The Ravenglass estuary is a haunt of wildfowl and waders. Oyster-catchers and curlews probe the mudflats and there are sometimes raucous flocks of gulls. On Muncaster Fell there may be grouse in the heather and buzzards circling overhead.

Don't forget to explore the little village of Ravenglass. It's essentially a fishing village at the confluence of the rivers Irt, Mite and Esk. Apart from being a Roman port, by 1280 it had charters for a weekly market and annual fair, though its trade was eclipsed as the port of Whitehaven developed. As trade diminished, it became a centre for rum smuggling.

4 The path roughly follows the edge of a coniferous plantation. At the end of the plantation, the summit of **Muncaster Fell** is visible above and to the left, but the main path continues slightly to the right.

5 Keep right again at the next fork. The path meanders to avoid bogs and remain roughly level, with good views over **Eskdale**. Eventually a panorama of fells opens up at the curious structure known as **Ross's Camp**, a large stone slab which was turned into a picnic table for a shooting party in 1883.

6 Continue along the footpath, looping deviously round a broad boggy area to reach a corner of a dry-stone wall. Go down through a gateway. The houses of **Eskdale Green** appear through a gap in the ridge, with **Scafell** rising behind. Descend (it's nearly always wet), keeping fairly close to the wall, until a drier path bears right across the dip through bracken and scattered trees. Make a short ascent on a well-buttressed stretch, then descend sparsely wooded slopes, through a gate, ending on a track near another gate.

Muncaster Castle is on the route of the walk

2h30	6 MILES	9.7 KM	LEVEL 1 2 3

MAP: OS Explorer OL 6 The English Lakes (SW)

START: car park at Ravenglass, close to station; grid ref: SD 085964.

FINISH: Eskdale Green Station; grid ref: SD 145998

PATHS: clear tracks and paths, muddy after rain, 1 stile

LANDSCAPE: woodland, moderately rugged fell and gentle valley

PUBLIC TOILETS: Ravenglass village and Ravenglass and Eskdale Station

TOURIST INFORMATION: Egremont, tel 01946 820693

THE PUB: King George IV Inn, Eskdale Green, near the end of the route

🛈 Moderately rough descents and wet ground likely. Suitability: children 8+

Getting to the start

Ravenglass is right on the coast, south of Seascale, accessed via a turn-off from the A595. Follow this road down into the village and the signed car park.

Researched and written by:
Paddy Dillon, Jon Sparks

7 Go through the gate and turn left, to a prominent **boulder**, then bear right to the end of a wall under some trees. A clear path follows the wall, then bears slightly right and down to a **stream**. Follow the narrow track beyond, joining a wider

track just below the railway. Follow the track almost to the road, then turn sharp left to reach **Eskdale Green Station**. Or, to find the **King George IV Inn**, turn right along the road for 300yds (274m).

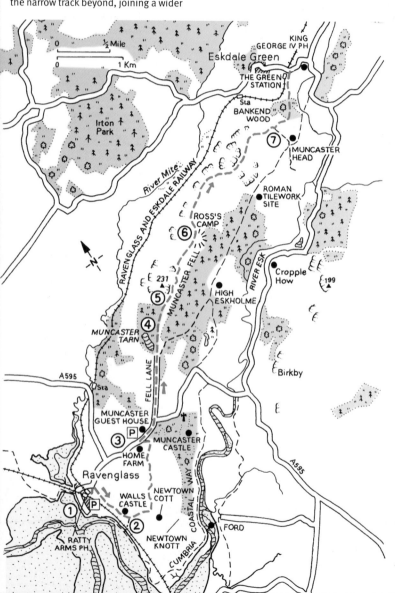

King George IV Inn

about the pub

King George IV Inn
Eskdale Green, Holmrook
Cumbria CA19 1TS
Tel 019467 23262
www.kinggeorge-iv.co.uk

DIRECTIONS: 300yds (274m) from the end of the walk, east of Eskdale Green Station	
PARKING: 5	
OPEN: daily, all day	
FOOD: daily, all day in summer	
BREWERY/COMPANY: free house	
REAL ALE: Coniston Bluebird, 3 guest beers	
DOGS: welcome in the bar	
ROOMS: 3 en suite	

Just a short stroll down the lane from The Green, this 17th-century coaching inn is located at the heart of one of Lakeland's finest hidden valleys, close to picturesque Dalegarth Falls. Inside, a rambling series of character bars have open fires, oak beams, low ceilings and flagged floors, with antiques to browse among before you eat. There is a good range of real ales and a huge selection of almost 200 malt whiskies available. Two outside seating areas – front and rear – both have expansive fell views. The front tables are a particular suntrap in the mornings and the rear garden incorporates a gravelled area with decking.

Food
Home-cooked food includes Cumberland sausage and egg, pan-fried liver and onions, steak and ale pie, seafood casserole, lamb shank in red wine and rosemary, and a range of steaks. Good vegetarian selection and traditional lunchtime snacks.

Family facilities
Children are welcome inside and there's a menu for younger diners.

Alternative refreshment stops
The Ratty Arms is in the old mainline railway station at Ravenglass. Families are welcome and meals are provided.

☞ Where to go from here
About 1 mile (1.6km) east of Ravenglass is Muncaster Castle, a privately owned mansion dating back to 1200 and headquarters of the World Owl Trust.

The scenic view from the terrace gardens of Muncaster Castle

High around Loweswater Fell

A circuit from Low Lorton to Loweswater and back through Lorton Vale.

Alien invaders

Signs on this route draw attention to the peril of red squirrels in the area. The red squirrel is native to Britain but over the last century or so has been widely displaced by the grey squirrel, introduced from North America. Red squirrels have longer bodies and tails than the greys but a much more slender build and are considerably lighter. Today there are an estimated 2.5 million greys to just 160,000 reds, and most of those are found in Scotland. Around 30,000 red squirrels survive in England and Wales, mainly in Cumbria and Northumberland.

The rhododendrons which make such a splash on the fellside above Loweswater are also an introduced species, this time from the Himalayas. Spectacular in bloom, they are tough, hardy mountain plants and thrive in the acid soils and cool, moist climate of the Lake District. The snag is that, rather like the grey squirrel, they tend to compete all too well with native plant species and if left unchecked can displace native shrubs and flowering plants over large areas. In some areas you may see conservation volunteers working to cut them back – but it is a mammoth task.

the ride

1 Follow the road down to the bridge over the **River Cocker** and round to the right. Shortly after, turn left on a road marked 'Unsuitable for motor vehicles'. This begins to climb almost at once and goes on for about 0.5 mile (800m). The steepest section goes through a tunnel of trees between **Low Bank Farm** and **High Bank**.

View towards Crummock Water from the lane above Thackthwaite

The beautiful view from the shores of Loweswater

2h00 · **9.75 MILES** · **15.7 KM** · **LEVEL 123 3**

MAP:	OS Explorer OL 4 The English Lakes (NW)
START/FINISH:	outskirts of Low Lorton; grid ref: NY 1532577
TRAILS/TRACKS:	quiet lanes, moderately rough tracks with some potholes
LANDSCAPE:	woodland, waterside, gentle valley, rough grazing land and moorland
PUBLIC TOILETS:	none on route
TOURIST INFORMATION:	Cockermouth, tel 01900 822634
CYCLE HIRE:	Keswick Mountain Bikes, tel 017687 75202; Grin Up North, Cockermouth, tel 01900 829600
THE PUB:	Wheatsheaf Inn, Low Lorton, see Point **1** on route

🛈 One very steep climb. Lengthy off-road descents, but not too difficult. Suitability: children 11+

Getting to the start

Low Lorton lies bewteen Cockermouth and Keswick, off the B5292. Park on wide verges near a phone-box on the B5289, just south of Lorton Hall.

Why do this cycle ride?

This ride has its challenges, including a tough climb early on, but you are repaid. There are fine views, first out over the Cumbrian lowlands to the Solway Firth and the hills of Galloway, in Scotland, then over Loweswater and its encircling fells, and finally up into the heart of the Lake District. There is some wonderful traffic-free riding on good tracks, and two exhilarating descents. These are never difficult, but to enjoy them fully you do need confidence in yourself and your bike.

Researched and written by: Jon Sparks

CYCLE

Low Lorton CUMBRIA

2 Above this the gradient gradually eases. At the same time the surface becomes progressively rougher. This shouldn't pose any problems as long as you keep an eye on the track ahead and pick your moments to look round at the views. And these are great, over **Cockermouth** to the **Solway Firth** and the Galloway hills. There's one more short climb before the lane starts to dip downhill. The descent never gets too steep or too difficult, as long as you keep a good lookout for potholes. This run down levels out over tiny **Catgill Bridge** and brings you to a T-junction onto a road.

3 Turn left and wind past the fine buildings of **Mosser Mains**, just beyond which the road forks. Take the left branch, which climbs gradually up the valley of **Mosser Beck**. There's a steeper section just before **Mossergate Farm**. Once past High Mossergate, the surface again gets rougher as the gradient eases. As the track levels out, the high Lakeland fells begin to appear ahead. Pass the narrow **Graythwaite Wood** (mostly rhododendrons, giving an outlandish splash of colour in early summer) at the start of another swooping descent.

4 The track swings left, traversing a steep hillside above **Loweswater**. The surface is generally better on the steepest part of the descent, although there are still a few potholes. Continue along a rougher section, at a gentler gradient, through a **plantation** and finally down to meet the road just above the lake.

5 Bear left along the road. There's a short climb as the road veers away from the lake, followed by a slight descent and then a more level section. Crest another slight rise and there's a view of **Crummock Water** and the high fells, with **Great Gable** a prominent rounded peak in the distance. Just a short way down the other side is a turning on the left, signposted to Thackthwaite, and also a **C2C sign**.

6 Turn here and follow this narrow lane through the tiny hamlet of **Thackthwaite**, where a sign says, 'Red Squirrels Please drive slowly' (I'm sure they do!). The lane is undulating but predominantly downhill, bringing you gradually down to the valley floor alongside the beck, past the **caravan park** at Whin Fell and on to a T-junction. Turn right over the bridge to return to the start point.

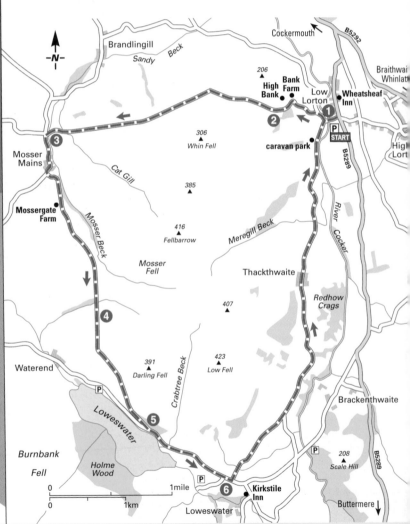

Wheatsheaf Inn

Long, low and white, this 17th-century inn sits squarely along the main road through Low Lorton, just a short way from the start and finish of the ride. The bar, with beams and log fire, is decorated with books and memorabilia to resemble a gamekeeper's lodge. There's another open fire in the non-smoking restaurant. To the rear is a large, safe garden with fine views to the fells, and the pub has a caravan site. There's a selection of beer from the Jennings brewery in nearby Cockermouth, and good food is a high priority, sourced locally if possible.

Food

A typical menu may include mussels in white wine and garlic sauce or home-made soup to start, followed by beef and beer pie, duck breast with orange marmalade, half shoulder of lamb with Cumberland sauce, or a large Yorkshire pudding filled with roast beef. Good fish specials and lighter lunchtime snacks.

Family facilities

Families are welcome inside and there are specific menus for younger children and

about the pub

Wheatsheaf Inn
Low Lorton, Cockermouth
Cumbria CA13 9UW
Tel 01900 85199
www.wheatsheafinnlorton.co.uk

DIRECTIONS: on the B5289, between Low Lorton and Lorton Hall

PARKING: 40

OPEN: daily in summer, closed Monday lunch October to May

FOOD: daily

BREWERY/COMPANY: Jennings Brewery

REAL ALE: Jennings Bitter, Cumberland Ale and seasonal beers

---

for teenagers. Extensive rear garden for summer eating and drinking.

Alternative refreshment stops

Close to Point 6, in Loweswater village, you'll find the Kirkstile Inn (good food and home-brewed beer).

☞ Where to go from here

Wordworth's childhood home in the riverside town of Cockermouth is well worth a visit. Next door there is a working printing museum, The Printing House, with an interesting range of historic presses and equipment. At the Lakeland Sheep and Wool Centre children can see 19 different breeds of sheep, as well as shearing demonstrations and sheepdog trials. Alternatively, enjoy a tour of the Jennings Brewery.

Loweswater

Loweswater

CUMBRIA

Discovering Lakeland's finest natural balcony in a little-trodden corner of the north western Fells.

Loweswater

Loweswater is one of Lakeland's finest yet least talked about lakes – perhaps because it's a bit remote from the more popular parts of Lakeland. Mention it to your friends and 'Where's Loweswater then?' is the likely response. Well, it's that lake beyond Buttermere and Crummock Water, the one people never quite get around to visiting.

Loweswater village is little more than the Kirkstile Inn, the church and the village hall, with a scattering of whitewashed farm buildings in the lush green fields and alongside the narrow country lanes. The walk starts on the outskirts of the village, by Maggie's Bridge. It uses an old 'corpse road' to get to the fellsides. The corpses? They would have been parishioners from Loweswater, for the church didn't have its own burial ground. They would be strapped on to horses' backs before being carried all the way to St Bees on the coast. After the climb up the high sides of Carling Knott, the mourners might not have appreciated that this is one of the most splendid balcony paths in Cumbria – green, flat and true – and with wonderful views across the lake to Darling Fell.

The old track descends to farm pastures. The names of the farmhouses – Iredale Place, Jenkinson Place and Hudson Place – are all derived from the original owners' names. Beyond the last-mentioned, the route comes down to the lake. Loweswater is celebrated among anglers

Sheep grazing in the lush green fields near Loweswater

for its trout and its perch. Both fish are hunted down by the predatory pike, a huge streamlined fish present here in large numbers.

the walk

1 Just opposite the car park entrance go through a gate marked **High Nook** and follow the track through the fields. After passing through the farmyard, keep left of the beck and follow a stony track that climbs into the comb of **Highnook Beck** below the craggy sides of **Carling Knott**.

WALK

2 Take the right fork each time the path divides. This brings you down to a small footbridge over the stream. Across the bridge the route continues as a fine grassy track that doubles back right, raking across the hillside to the top of the **Holme Wood plantations**. The track follows the top edge of the woods before traversing the breast of **Burnbank Fell**.

3 The track swings left and climbs to a **ladder stile** and a gate to the north of the fell. Go over the stile and follow the track, descending gradually across rough grazing land.

4 A couple of hundred paces short of the road at **Fangs Brow**, turn right over a ladder stile (signed to Loweswater via Hudson Place) and follow a rutted track to just above **Iredale Place farm**. Keep right, along a tarmac lane.

Loweswater, surrounded by green hills

MAP: OS Explorer OL 4 The English Lakes (NW)
START/FINISH: Maggie's Bridge car park, Loweswater; grid ref: NY 134210
PATHS: well-defined paths and tracks, all stiles have adjacent gates
LANDSCAPE: hillside, farm pastures, forest and lakes
PUBLIC TOILETS: none on route
TOURIST INFORMATION: Cockermouth, tel 01900 822634
THE PUB: Kirkstile Inn, Loweswater, 0.5 mile (800m) off route
Suitability: children 6+

Getting to the start

The hamlet of Loweswater lies between the small lake of Loweswater and the northern tip of Crummock Water. Maggie's Bridge car park (arrive early for a place) is down a very narrow lane, 0.5 mile (800m) west of the church and the Kirkstile Inn.

Researched and written by:
John Gillham, Jon Sparks

Loweswater CUMBRIA

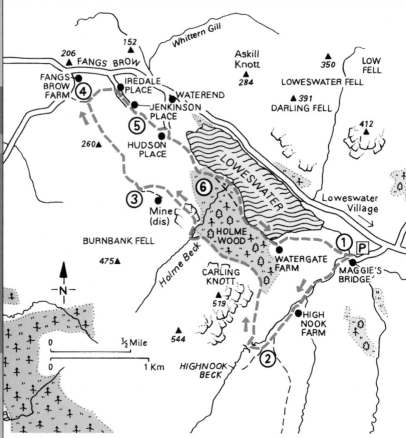

5 On reaching **Jenkinson Place** (a farm) the tarmac lane ends. Follow the stony track beyond for a short way, then turn left,

what to look for

There's been a place of worship at Loweswater since 1158 when Ranulph de Lyndesay gave a chapel and some land to the Abbey of St Bees. In 1827 that building was demolished to make way for the present (much larger) church, for lead mining had increased the local population to over 500 at this time. At the same time a school for 80 children was built – it's now the village hall.

over a stile. Follow a well-defined grass track across fields and along a line of hawthorn trees. At **Hudson Place** follow the signed path skirting around the farm complex to meet a lane. Turn right and follow the lane, which nears the shores of **Loweswater** before entering **Holme Wood**.

6 A wide track now heads through the woods, but by taking a path to the left you can get nearer the shoreline. This second path rejoins the original track just beyond a stone-built hut, or bothy. At **Watergate Farm** turn left to follow a wide gravel road back to the **car park** at Maggie's Bridge.

Kirkstile Inn

Family facilities
Children are welcome in the bars and dining room and have their own menu. The peaceful garden is well away from the road.

☛ Where to go from here
Follow the B5289 past Buttermere and over the Honister Pass to Borrowdale to view the Bowder Stone and Ladore Falls. Then continue to Keswick and step aboard a launch to explore Derwent Water, or learn about Keswick's industrial past at the Keswick Museum and Gallery.

Although the Kirkstile Inn is 0.5 mile (800m) off the route it's worth the detour, or return to your car and drive to it. This characterful inn has been providing hospitality for over 400 years and enjoys a beautiful position beside the tumbling waters of Park Beck and the base of Mellbreak, with views stretching over Crummock Water to the massive, seamed bulk of Grasmoor. Ultimately, it's a super spot to enjoy a jar of home-brewed ale. Expect a classic Lakeland pub interior, with original beams, cushioned settles and pews, thick stone walls and a blazing log fire – very inviting after a day on the hills. Walkers are made very welcome, however wet or muddy they are! The Kirkstile Inn is one of the best pubs in the Lakes.

Food
High quality food – a succulent steak with a green peppercorn and mustard sauce, steak, mushroom and pink peppercorn pie, baked monkfish – is complemented by an extensive, reasonably priced wine list. A good range of sandwiches, soups and filled baguettes, too.

about the pub

Kirkstile Inn
Loweswater, Cockermouth
Cumbria CA13 0RU
Tel 01900 85219
www.kirkstile.com

DIRECTIONS: by the church in the hamlet	
PARKING: 30	
OPEN: daily, all day	
FOOD: daily	
BREWERY/COMPANY: free house	
REAL ALE: Jennings Cumberland Ale, Yates's Bitter, guest beer	
DOGS: welcome in the bar	
ROOMS: 11 bedrooms (9 en suite)	

A circuit from Wast Water to Stanton Bridge

CYCLE

Wast Water

CUMBRIA

A pleasant rural ride with a short option and a magnificent scenic finale.

Wast Water

Wast Water is England's deepest lake, reaching a maximum depth of almost 26oft (79m), which means that its bed is well below sea level. The steep slope of The Screes, which face you across the lake, is continued deep underwater. The Screes, below the two summits of Whin Rigg and Illgill Head, are composed of decaying crags and masses of loose rock and boulders. This is landscape that is still evolving. There is a path, which you may be able to make out, running along the base of The Screes just above the level of the lake. It is no surprise to find that it is extremely rough going in places.

Looking up to the head of the lake and at the centre of the view (and of the National Park logo) is the pyramidal peak of Great Gable, 2,949ft (899m) high. High on its slopes facing you are the Napes Crags, beloved of the earliest rock-climbers and

Left: Cyclists on the route above Wast Water
Page 43: Scafell and Great Gable

of generations since. But only with very sharp eyes, or binoculars, and even then only in favourable light, are you likely to discern the natural obelisk called Napes Needle. Its first ascent in 1886 is often regarded as the birth of rock-climbing. It features in a memorial window in the lovely little church at Wasdale Head.

the ride

1 Head west along the road towards **Gosforth**, climbing slightly and passing close under the craggy slopes of **Buckbarrow**. Climb a little more and then descend to a junction.

2 For the shorter loop, go left here, signed for Nether Wasdale. Follow the narrow lane and descend to a junction. Keep left and descend quite steeply into **Nether Wasdale**, levelling out at the village green, with **The Screes Inn** on the left and the **Strands Hotel** on the right (Point 5). For the longer ride, continue straight ahead at Point 2 and go straight on at the next junction. The road is fairly level, with views over the valley of the **River Irt** to the left and wooded slopes on the right. A little over 1 mile (1.6km) from the last junction, look for a bridleway on the left, signed for Hall Bolton.

3 Turn left onto the bridleway. The initial descent from the road is as rough as it gets. Keep right where the track forks and go straight ahead between the buildings at **Rainors**. Wind down to an attractive bridge over the **River Bleng**. Beyond this there's a short grassy section, then join the surfaced drive to **Hall Bolton**. Turn right and follow the drive out to a road. Turn left. Note, this track is rarely very muddy, but after wet weather you risk a soaking on the grassy section beyond the bridge. To avoid this, continue along the road at Point 3 over a small climb and then down steeply to **Wellington Bridge** and the outskirts of **Gosforth**. Bear left on a farm lane (bridleway) through **Row Farm** and on to **Rowend Bridge**. Turn left to follow the road to Santon Bridge. This adds about 1 mile (1.6km) to the total distance. Follow the road easily to **Santon Bridge**, past the pub and over the bridge.

4 Turn left on a narrow road past a campsite and soon begin a steeper climb at **Greengate Wood**. The gradient eases and the views ahead start to include the craggy outline of **The Screes**. Descend gently to **Forest Bridge**, then keep left, over **Cinderdale Bridge**, into **Nether Wasdale**. Follow the level road into the village and its twin pubs.

5 Retrace to **Cinderdale Bridge**, then keep left on the lane, signed to Wasdale Head. There are glimpses of The Screes and then of the lake, but trees screen them as you pass the youth hostel at **Wasdale Hall** and it's only when you cross a cattle grid to open fellside that the full panorama hits you. Follow the road down and then up a short climb to near a **cross-wall shelter** on the right, which commands a great view.

6 Continue down to cross **Countess Beck** and turn left. It's now little more than 0.25 mile (400m) back to the start.

2h00 — **11.25 MILES** — **18.1 KM** — **LEVEL 1 2 3**

SHORTER ALTERNATIVE ROUTE

1h00 — **5 MILES** — **8 KM** — **LEVEL 1 2 3**

MAP: OS Explorer OL 6 The English Lakes (SW)

START/FINISH: by Wast Water, roadside parking at Greendale; grid ref: NY 144057

TRAILS/TRACKS: lanes; longer route has a short section of grassy bridleway

LANDSCAPE: wooded farmland then open fellside with view of lake and high fells

PUBLIC TOILETS: Gosforth

TOURIST INFORMATION: Ravenglass, tel 01229 717278; Sellafield, tel 019467 76510

CYCLE HIRE: Ainfield Cycle Centre, Cleator, tel 01946 812427; Mark Taylor Cycles, Whitehaven, tel 01946 692252

THE PUB: The Screes Inn, Nether Wasdale, see Point **5** on route

🛈 Some ascents and descents on both routes. Shorter loop, suitability: children 8+. Longer loop, suitability: children 11+

Getting to the start

Head east from Gosforth, pass a car park, then keep left on the Wasdale road. Follow this for 3 miles (4.8km) then keep left, signed to Wasdale Head for 2.5 miles (4km). Park in a grassy area on the left just past Greendale.

Why do this cycle ride?

The magnificent view of high fells around the head of Wast Water inspired the Lake District National Park logo, and would win many votes for the finest view in England. The ride saves this until near the end, first exploring the gentler scenery around Nether Wasdale.

Researched and written by: Jon Sparks

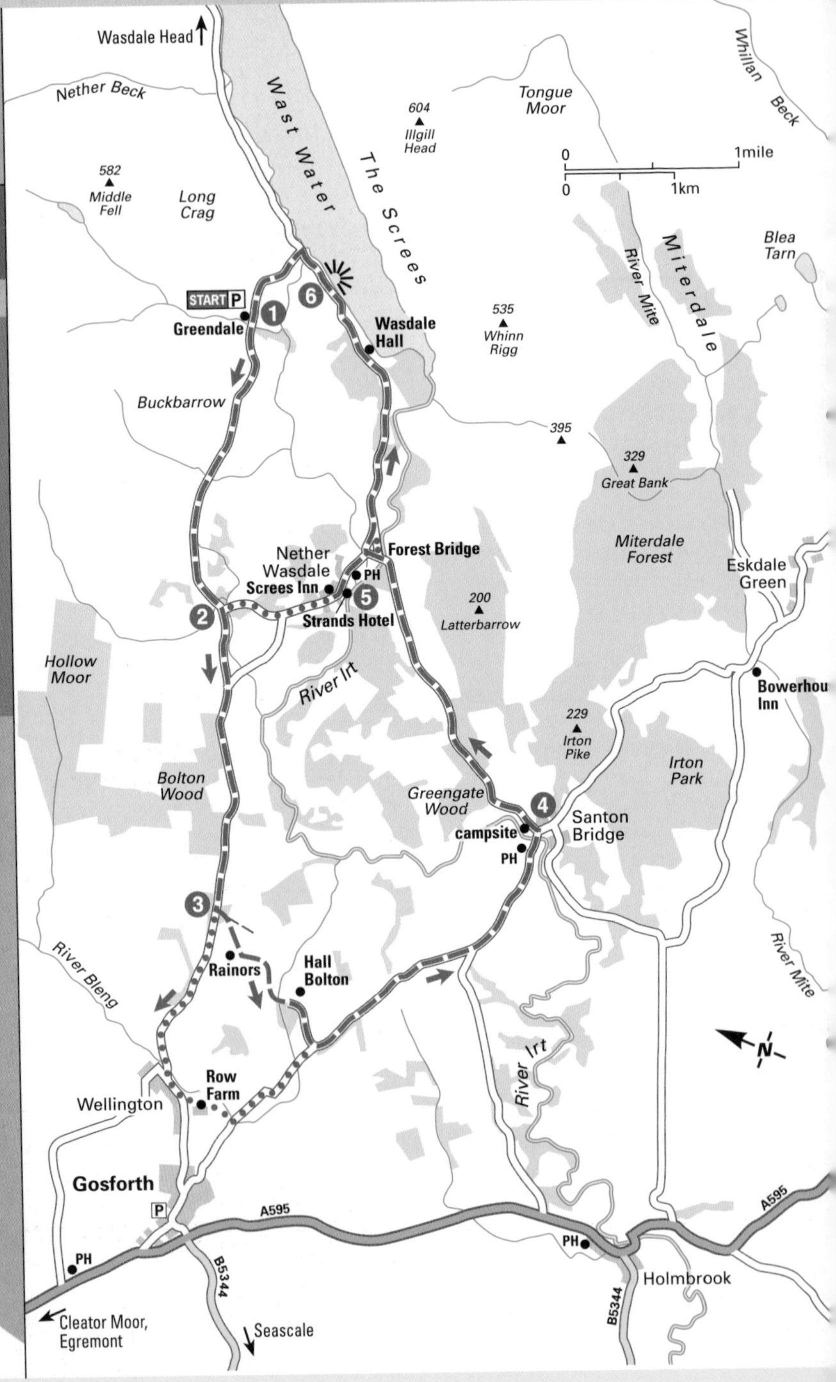

Wast Water   CUMBRIA

Wasdale Head ↑

Nether Beck

West Water

The Screes

Whillan Beck

Tongue Moor

604 ▲ Illgill Head

582 ▲ Middle Fell

Long Crag

0   1mile
0   1km

Blea Tarn

START P ① ⑥

Greendale

Wasdale Hall

535 ▲ Whinn Rigg

River Mite

Miterdale

Buckbarrow

395 ▲

329 ▲ Great Bank

Nether Wasdale
Screes Inn

Forest Bridge

PH

⑤

Strands Hotel

②

Miterdale Forest

Eskdale Green

Hollow Moor

River Irt

200 ▲ Latterbarrow

229 ▲ Irton Pike

Bowerhou Inn

Bolton Wood

Greengate Wood

④ Santon Bridge

Irton Park

campsite
PH

③

River Bleng

Rainors

Hall Bolton

River Irt

Row Farm

Wellington

Gosforth
P

A595

PH

Cleator Moor, Egremont

B5344

Seascale

PH

Holmbrook

B5344

A595

N

42

The Screes Inn

about the pub

The Screes Inn
Nether Wasdale, Seascale
Cumbria CA20 1ET
Tel 019467 26262
www.thescreesinnwasdale.com

DIRECTIONS: on the main road through the village, west of the church

PARKING: 20

OPEN: daily, all day

FOOD: daily

BREWERY/COMPANY: free house

REAL ALE: Black Sheep Bitter, Coniston Bluebird, Yates's Bitter, guest beer

ROOMS: 5 en suite

Two pubs face each other across the lane through Nether Wasdale, but both are owned by the same people. To pick one over the other may be invidious, but the 300-year-old Screes Inn does have one or two advantages: it's easy to park your bikes in sight of the outdoor tables, and it's open all day. Outside seating is separated from the road by an expanse of grass – a sort of village green – with a sunny aspect and glimpses of the fells lining Wasdale. Inside, it's a typically rambling Lakeland pub. The bars are partly slate-floored, and there's usually a log fire crackling in the grate – the perfect spot to savour a pint of Yates's bitter. Bike storage for overnight visitors.

Food

Specials from the blackboard might include smoked haddock, leek and potato pasties or Mexican wraps. Alternatively, try Woodall's Cumberland sausage with apple sauce, lasagne or home-baked steak and kidney pie. Vegetarians will always be well looked after as The Screes has a vegetarian chef.

Family facilities

Families will find a separate family room for the children to relax in. Small portions of main menu dishes are available (young children have their own menu), and there is plenty of good outdoor seating.

Alternative refreshment stops

The Strands Hotel in Nether Wasdale and, on the longer ride, the Bridge Inn at Stanton Bridge.

☛ Where to go from here

St Olaf's Church at Wasdale Head is one of England's smallest, and in its cemetery are the graves of several rock-climbers; this village became known as the birthplace of rock-climbing in Britain in the 1880s.

WALK

Around Buttermere

A relaxing walk in one of Lakeland's most attractive valleys.

Buttermere

Much has been written about lovely Buttermere – the dale, the village and the lake. The area achieved considerable notoriety at the pen of Joseph Budworth, who stayed here in 1792 and encountered Mary, the daughter of the landlord of the Fish Inn. In his guidebook *Fortnight's Ramble to the Lakes*, he described Mary as 'the reigning Lily of the Valley', and the unfortunate woman became a tourist attraction.

In 1802 the tale brought to Buttermere one John Hadfield, a man posing as the Honourable Anthony Augustus Hope, MP. Hadfield wooed and won Mary, and they were married at Lorton church on 2 October 1802 (coincidentally just two days before William Wordsworth married Mary Hutchinson). With the honeymoon scarcely begun, however, Hadfield was exposed as an impostor and arrested on a charge of forgery – a more serious offence than that of bigamy, of which he was also guilty. He was later tried and hanged at Carlisle. The whole saga was dramatised and found its way on to the stages of some London theatres. Accounts of the episode are given by Thomas de Quincey in *Recollections of the Lakes and the Lake Poets* and by Melvyn Bragg in his 1987 novel *The Maid of Buttermere*, and a description used by Wordsworth in 'The Prelude'. As for Mary, she later remarried, had a large family and by all accounts a subsequently happy life.

the walk

1 Leave the car park and turn right, passing the **Fish Hotel** to follow a broad track through gates. Ignore the signposted route to Scale Force and continue along the track towards the edge of the lake. Then follow the line of a hedgerow to a bridge at **Buttermere Dubs**. Cross over and bear left, passing just below the foot of the cascade of **Sourmilk Gill**. Cross a smaller footbridge and go through a gate into **Burtness Wood**. Bear left on a track through the woods that roughly parallels the lakeshore, finally emerging from the trees near **Horse Close**, where a bridge spans **Comb Beck**.

2 Keep on along the path to reach a wall leading to a sheepfold and a gate. Go left through the gate, cross **Warnscale Beck** and walk out to **Gatesgarth Farm**. At the farm, follow signs to reach the valley

Left: Hikers gazing across Buttermere
Below: Ducks on the shore of Crummock Water

road (the **B5289**). Turn left on the road for about 500yds (457m) until it meets the **lakeshore**. For much of this distance there are no pathways: take care against approaching traffic.

3 As the road leaves the lakeshore again, leave it for a **footpath** on the left signposted 'Buttermere via Lakeshore Path'. The path leads into a field, beyond which it never strays far from the shoreline and continues to a stand of Scots pine, near **Crag Wood**.

4 Beyond **Hassnesshow Beck bridge**, the path enters the grounds of Hassness, where a rocky path, enclosed by trees, leads to a gate. Here a path has been cut across a crag dropping into the lake below, and shortly disappears into a brief, low and damp **tunnel**, unique in the Lake District. The tunnel was cut by employees of George Benson, a 19th-century Manchester mill owner who then owned the Hassness Estate, to enable him to walk around the lake without straying too far from its shore. After you emerge from the tunnel a gate gives access to a gravel path across the wooded pasture of **Pike Rigg**. Where a permitted path goes left to stay by the lakeshore, the main path keeps straight ahead, crossing a traditional Lakeland bridge of slate slabs.

2h00 — **4.5 MILES** — **7.2 KM** — **LEVEL 1** 23

MAP: OS Explorer OL 4 The English Lakes (NW)

START/FINISH: Buttermere, National Park car park beyond Fish Hotel (fee); grid ref: NY 173169

PATHS: good paths, some road walking, 2 stiles

LANDSCAPE: lakeside, fells, woodland and farmland

PUBLIC TOILETS: at start

TOURIST INFORMATION: Keswick, tel 017687 72645

THE PUB: Bridge Hotel, Buttermere, see Point **5** on route

🛈 Suitability: children 5+

Getting to the start

Buttermere village lies between the lakes of Buttermere and Crummock Water, on the B5289. Approaching from the south, pass Buttermere church and turn left before the Bridge Hotel. The car park is to the right of the Fish Hotel.

Researched and written by:
Terry Marsh, Jon Sparks

5 A short way on, through another gate, the path leads on to **Wilkinsyke Farm**, and an easy walk out to the road, just a short way above the **Bridge Hotel**. Turn left to return to the car park.

what to look for

While walking out to Gatesgarth Farm, have a look at the craggy sides of Fleetwith Pike. On the lower slopes a white cross can be seen clearly. This was erected by the friends of Fanny Mercer, a luckless visitor to Lakeland who, in 1887, while out walking, tripped over her long walking pole and fell to her death.

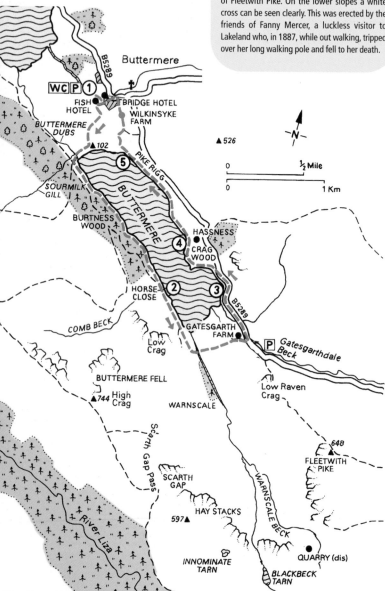

Bridge Hotel

Spend a weekend at this 18th-century former coaching inn and enjoy its stunning location in an area of outstanding natural beauty between Buttermere and Crummock Water. You can round off spectacular walks with afternoon tea, excellent ales or a hearty meal. On a fine day there can be fierce competition for tables in the small garden, a sheltered suntrap surrounded by climbing roses, with jaw-dropping views to High Crag, High Stile and Red Pike. What better place to enjoy a pint of Old Faithful from the (Cumbrian) Tirril Brewery? If the seats are all taken or the weather forces you indoors, there are two bar areas, one with oak beams, a flagstone floor and traditional Lakeland character. There's also a plush lounge with deep sofas and an open fire. Individually designed bedrooms.

Food

Main courses include Cumberland hotpot, home-made steak and kidney pie, vegetable stirfry, and deep-fried haddock in crisp beer batter. For smaller appetites there's a good selection of salads, sandwiches and toasties. Separate five-course dinner menu in the restaurant.

Family facilities

Children are welcome in the eating area of the bar; children's menu.

Alternative refreshment stops

There is a café at Buttermere and, like the Bridge Hotel, the Fish Inn serves teas, coffee, snacks and bar meals throughout the day. Wilkinsyke Farm does home-made ice cream and there's often a tea-wagon at Gatescarth.

☛ Where to go from here

Buttermere's attractive church of 1841 is in a superb position on a rocky knoll. It is tiny, with a bellcote and a lower chancel. From it there is a lovely view of the valley and the high fells on the south side, all the way to Hay Stacks.

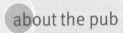

about the pub

Bridge Hotel
Buttermere
Cumbria CA13 9UZ
Tel 017687 70252
www.bridge-hotel.com

DIRECTIONS: in the centre of Buttermere village

PARKING: 26

OPEN: daily, all day

FOOD: daily, all day (restaurant evenings only)

BREWERY/COMPANY: free house

REAL ALE: Black Sheep Bitter, Theakston Old Peculier, Tirril Old Faithful

DOGS: welcome in garden only

ROOMS: 21 en suite

From Eskdale to Miterdale

Discovering peaceful hills that were once a Norman hunting preserve.

Eskdale

The area around Eskdale lay within the Norman barony of Copeland, a name which derives from the Old Norse 'kaupaland' meaning 'bought land', and was granted to William de Briquessart in the early 12th century. His hunting preserve, or 'forest', together with the neighbouring Derwentfells Forest, extended all the way from the Esk to the Derwent and remained under Forest Law for more than a century. The few peasants who lived within the forest bounds were subject to Draconian laws that affected almost every aspect of their meagre existence. The clearance of additional land for grazing or cultivation, known as 'assarting', was forbidden and it was illegal to allow cattle or sheep to stray into the forest. Felling a tree for timber to repair a cottage or fencing required special permission and even the collection of wood for fuel was strictly controlled.

The estate was policed by foresters, who were keen to bring malefactors before the forest courts for punishment. Penalties were often severe and ranged from a complex system of fines for minor infringements to flogging, mutilation or even death for poaching. Often near to starvation themselves, the commoners were required to assist as beaters, butchers and carriers for the hunts, and watch their overlords kill, perhaps, more than 100 deer in a single day. Yet if game animals broke through the fences around their allotments and destroyed the paltry crop, they were powerless to do anything other than chase them away.

The hunting preserve gradually diminished during the 13th century, as ever larger areas were turned over to sheep farming. Constant grazing has prevented the regeneration of natural woodland and left the open landscape now so characteristic of the area.

the walk

1 Follow the road down the valley. You can use a riverside path for a short way before **Beckfoot Bridge**. Cross the bridge and go up to the railway halt. Cross the line to a gate from where a zigzag path to **Blea Tarn** is signposted up the hillside. As the tarn appears, keep straight ahead on the clearest path, crossing the stream and leaving the tarn to your right.

2 The path rises slightly and bears right, runs level across a shoulder, then curves right again past tiny **Blind Tarn** and the larger, reedy **Siney Tarn**. Keep left, rounding the tarn, to a lone tree. Fork right just beyond the tree to cross a slight saddle. Follow an indistinct path down a slope dropping into **Miterdale** and bear left towards a **conifer plantation**. Descend steeply alongside this to an obvious track. Cross the track and negotiate a wet patch to cross a stile in a wire fence. Continue down parallel to the wall, usually keeping well right of it to avoid the worst bogs. The driest ground is where bracken grows. The wet surroundings support some wonderful plants, notably orchids, asphodel and the carnivorous sundew. Finally reach a well-made track just above the **River Mite**.

what to look for

Scattered across Brat's Moss are the remains of stone huts and a field system as well as five impressive circles of standing stones. They were erected during the Bronze Age, perhaps 5,500 years ago, and suggest quite a large settlement on what is now an almost desolate landscape.

3 Turn right and follow this track for about 400yds (366m) until it bends left through a **gateway**. Keep straight ahead on a less distinct track between a wall and a plantation until this, in turn, forks. The left branch goes down through a gap in the wall, but take the right, uphill, over a **stile** and steeply up beside the plantation to reach open fell at the top. Bear left, parallel to a wall.

4 Cross a beck (**Black Gill**) and continue towards a prominent boulder. Fork right again on a fainter path, passing some piles of stones, before bearing right across a slight dip to a couple of **low stone circles** and other remains. The path now rises to find two more imposing stone circles on the crest.

5 Bear right at the second circle, keep right past a wider circle and under a rocky outcrop. Go over a small rise, then fork left on a faint path past a large **cairn**. A group of **stone huts** comes into view. Below these a clear track descends right.

6 Follow it down **Boot Bank** and into Boot, and cross **Whillan Beck** by **Eskdale Mill** to continue past the **Burnmoor Inn**. At the end of the lane turn right to return to **Dalegarth Station**.

WALK

Eskdale CUMBRIA

3h00 · **5 MILES** · **8 KM** · **LEVEL 1 2 3**

MAP: OS Explorer OL 6 The English Lakes (SW)

START/FINISH: car park beside Dalegarth Station (pay-and-display); grid ref: NY 173007

PATHS: good paths in valleys, but often indistinct on hills, often wet, 3 stiles

LANDSCAPE: heath and moor with views across surrounding valleys

PUBLIC TOILETS: at Dalegarth Station

TOURIST INFORMATION: Egremont, tel 01946 820693

THE PUB: Burnmoor Inn, Boot, near end of route

🛑 Rough descents and wet ground likely. Navigation very tricky on open moor in poor visibility. Suitability: children 12+

Getting to the start

From Ambleside and other central Lakeland bases, the shortest route is west over Wrynose and Hardknott passes and then down through Eskdale to Dalegarth Station. From further afield, use the A595 to Duddon Bridge and up the Duddon Valley as far as Ulpha. About 0.25 mile (400m) past Ulpha post office turn left, cross Birker Fell and drop down into Eskdale to reach Dalegarth.

Researched and written by: Dennis Kelsall, Jon Sparks

Top left: View over Eskdale
Below: Siney Tarn

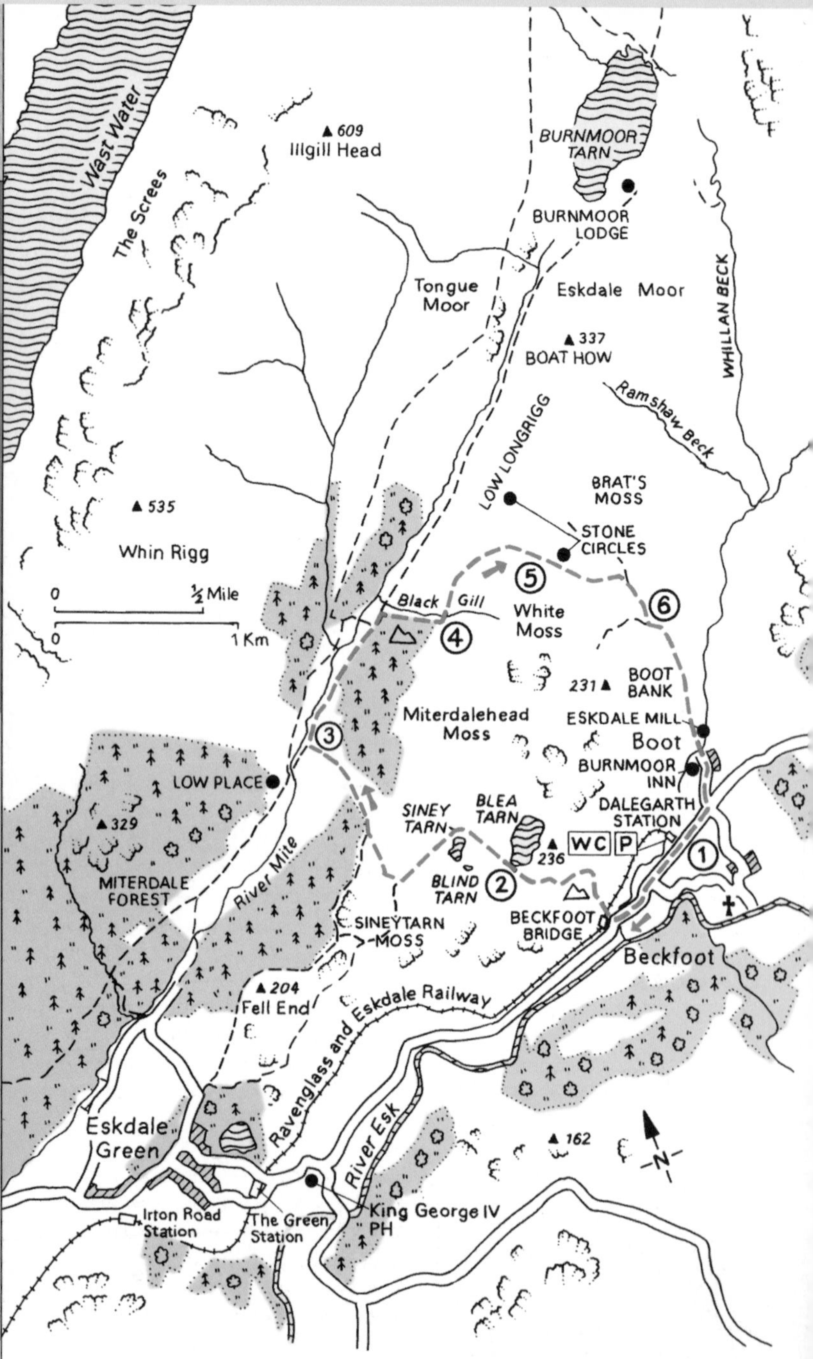

Wast Water

The Screes

▲ 609
Illgill Head

*BURNMOOR
TARN*

BURNMOOR
LODGE

WHILLAN BECK

Tongue
Moor

Eskdale Moor

▲ 337
BOAT HOW

Ramshaw Beck

LOW LONGRIGG

▲ 535

Whin Rigg

BRAT'S
MOSS

STONE
CIRCLES

⑤

⑥

0   ½ Mile

0   1 Km

Black Gill

④

White
Moss

④

BOOT
BANK

231 ▲

③

Miterdalehead
Moss

ESKDALE MILL

Boot

LOW PLACE

SINEY
TARN

BLEA
TARN

BURNMOOR
INN

DALEGARTH
STATION

▲ 329

River Mile

MITERDALE
FOREST

BLIND
TARN

②

W C P

236 ▲

①

SINEYTARN
MOSS

BECKFOOT
BRIDGE

✝

▲ 204
Fell End

Ravenglass and Eskdale Railway

Beckfoot

Eskdale
Green

River Esk

▲ 162

Irton Road
Station

The Green
Station

King George IV
PH

N

Burnmoor Inn

Situated at the foot of Scafell Pike, this traditional, comfortably modernised 16th-century inn attracts many hill walkers as well as visitors exploring beautiful Eskdale by car. A fire burns in the beamed bar in cooler weather, and there's a new conservatory and dining area with spectacular views of the western fells at any time of year. Cumbria ales take pride of place, but as many as 100 guest beers are also available through the course of a year . The garden, sheltered by mature pine trees, overlooks the quiet (dead-end) lane through the village, and catches the sun especially in the afternoon and evening – it's a great place to relax with a drink after this invigorating hill walk. Lovely en suite rooms for those wishing to stay.

about the pub

Burnmoor Inn
Boot, Eskdale Valley
Cumbria CA19 1TG
Tel 0845 1306224
www.burnmoor.co.uk

DIRECTIONS: just north of Dalegarth Station, at the end of the walk

PARKING: 30

OPEN: daily, all day

FOOD: daily (most of day)

BREWERY/COMPANY: free house

REAL ALE: Jennings Cumberland Ale, Yate's Bitter, guest ale

DOGS: well-behaved dogs welcome

ROOMS: 9 en suite

Food

Classic lunchtime pub food ranges from thick-cut sandwiches and Cumberland sausage to game stew and smoked haddock fishcakes. Evening options may take in roast pheasant.

Family facilities

The conservatory dining room makes a superb family room (own entrance) and children are welcome overnight. They can order small portions from the main menu and can use the swings in the spacious garden if they get bored with the fell views.

Alternative refreshment stops

There is a café at Dalegarth Station, but if you want something more substantial, call at the Brook House Inn in Boot.

☛ Where to go from here

A watermill still stands beside the packhorse bridge in Boot. It was built to grind corn in 1578 and worked by successive generations of the same family for almost 350 years. The mill has since been restored and is now open as a fascinating museum.

Seathwaite and the Duddon Valley

Follow in the footsteps
of the Romantic poet,
William Wordsworth.

Wordsworth and the Duddon Valley

William Wordsworth loved the Duddon
Valley so much that he wrote many sonnets
about it, including 'Hints for the Fancy from
the River Duddon' (1820). And little has
changed since his day. There's tarmac on
the winding walled lanes, but the byres
and woods and the lively stream that so
enthralled the poet are still there,
untouched for all to see.

The walk begins in Seathwaite, a remote
village with a rustic pub, a little church and a
handful of farms, set beneath the crags of
Wallowbarrow. A reservoir service road
takes the route easily up into the Coniston
Fells to the dam of Seathwaite Tarn. The
hushed waters of the large reservoir are
dwarfed by the rocks of Great Blake Rigg
and Buzzard Crag towering above.

Look the other way, and the jagged
cone of Harter Fell dominates the skyline
high above the forests, streams and
farmhouses. The route descends through
the heather and the bracken, and by a
chattering beck to the Duddon. Over the

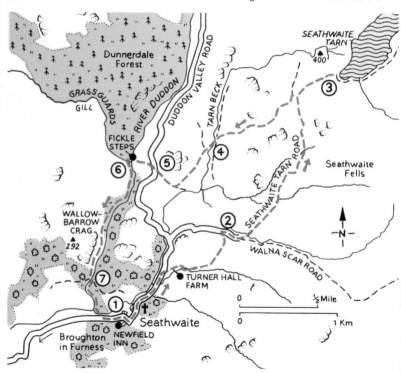

road, it comes to the Fickle Steps across the river. Wordsworth remembers them in a fanciful sonnet:

Not so that Pair whose youthful spirits dance
With Prompt emotion urging them to pass;
A sweet confusion checks the Shepherd lass;
Blushing she eyes the dizzy flood askance;
Too ashamed – too timid to advance

There's a wire across the river to steady your progress these days. It's an exciting prelude to a wonderful walk through the Wallowbarrow Gorge. From a lofty path you look down on the river and its bounding cataracts, then descend for a riverside stroll back into Seathwaite.

the walk

1 From **The Newfield Inn** at Seathwaite follow the road past the little church. In about 400yds (366m) turn right on the tarmac lane towards **Turner Hall Farm**, then take a track on the left signposted 'High Moss'. Keep left at a junction and follow the track to the isolated houses of **High Moss**. Skirt them on the left, go through a gate behind and follow the field path, ahead and then bearing left, out to the **Walna Scar Road**.

2 Turn right up the road. Where the tarmac ends turn left onto the utility company's access road to **Seathwaite Tarn**. This pleasant green track climbs steadily up the fellsides to the reservoir dam.

Left: The valley of Tarn Beck
Next page: Houses in Seathwaite, built of rocks from the surrounding area

3h00 | **5 MILES** | **8 KM** | **LEVEL 1 2 3**

MAP: OS Explorer OL 6 The English Lakes (SW)
START/FINISH: Seathwaite: roadside pull-off; grid ref: SD 231975, limited roadside parking near pub and church; grid ref: SD 228960
PATHS: paths, tracks, can be muddy below Seathwaite Tarn, 9 stiles
LANDSCAPE: craggy mountainside and wooded gorge
PUBLIC TOILETS: none on route
TOURIST INFORMATION: Broughton-in-Furness, tel 01229 716115
THE PUB: The Newfield Inn, Seathwaite, see Point 1 on route

 River crossing by stepping stones, too far apart for younger children; also rough slopes above river. If river is low it may be possible for children to paddle, otherwise return to Seathwaite along road. Suitability: children 11+ in typical conditions but very dependent on water level

Getting to the start

Seathwaite is on a minor road, 3 miles (4.8km) north of Ulpha and south of the Hardknott Pass. There are a few roadside parking spaces before the village (do not use those directly outside the pub), and a small lay-by opposite the church. If all these are full, continue for almost 1 mile (1.6km) to larger grassy spaces where the road reaches open fellside (Point 5 on the walk).

Researched and written by:
Dennis Kelsall, Jon Sparks

WALK

Seathwaite CUMBRIA

Seathwaite

CUMBRIA

3 Retrace your steps for 400yds (366m) to a waymarked post highlighting a downhill path, faint at first, that weaves through rock and rough pasture and steeply down beside a mountain stream. Cross a gate/stile, continue to another gate, and then cross a ladder stile to the banks of **Tarn Beck**.

4 Cross the footbridge and turn left. Follow a footpath along the lower edge of a wood. Pass behind a cottage and continue along to a ladder stile. Skirt a very wet area, then go through a gap in the wall and climb up to the **Duddon Valley road**.

5 Across the road follow the signed bridleway to the **Fickle Steps**, huge boulders which enable you to cross the River Duddon. Caution: if the river is high and the steps are awash, do not cross. The steps are too far apart for younger children to negotiate safely but it may be possible to paddle if the river is low. If there is any doubt, return by the road. (A footpath which starts opposite the church allows you to visit Wallowbarrow Gorge from the other end.)

6 Assuming you have crossed safely, turn left on the riverside path. Cross a footbridge over **Grassguards Gill**. The path gradually pulls away from the river, then traverses steep slopes above the tight wooded **Wallowbarrow Gorge**, before descending again to cross boulder-strewn terrain on the bank of the **River Duddon**, eventually reaching an arched stone footbridge.

7 Cross the bridge and turn right, following the east bank of the Duddon, to meet a tributary, **Tarn Beck**. Go up to a footbridge and cross to a short track out to the road. Turn left to return to **Seathwaite**.

what to look for

You will see clumps of bog myrtle in the peat meadows of the Duddon Valley, especially near the end of the walk. It's a low aromatic shrub with woody stems and oval leaves and it thrives in this marshy terrain. The branches have been used in past centuries, both for flavouring beer and for discouraging flies and midges, which apparently don't appreciate its eucalyptus-like scent.

The Newfield Inn

Located in Wordsworth's favourite – Duddon Valley – this unassuming 17th-century inn is understandably popular with walkers and climbers, with many good walks starting close to its door. 'Tardis-like' inside, the bar area has a magnificent slate floor, rustic wooden tables, a real fire, tip-top real ales, and a small collection of historic photographs. Slate floors are common enough in Cumbrian pubs but this is one of the best – it's still polite to get the worst of the mud off your boots first, though! On a good day the garden, tucked away at the back, is idyllic. Bask in the sun and gaze up at the Coniston Fells while the kids let off steam in the adjacent paddock.

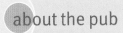

about the pub

The Newfield Inn
Seathwaite, Duddon Valley
Broughton-in-Furness
Cumbria LA20 6ED
Tel 01229 716208
www.newfieldinn.co.uk

DIRECTIONS: in Newfield, south west of the church

PARKING: 30

OPEN: daily, all day

FOOD: daily, all day

BREWERY/COMPANY: free house

REAL ALE: Daleside Bitter, Jennings Cumberland Ale, Theakston Old Peculier, guest beer

DOGS: well-behaved dogs on leads welcome inside

If the weather's less clement, a blazing fire will warm the cockles – helped along, perhaps, by a glass or two of Theakston's legendary Old Peculier ale.

Food
The menu encompasses home-made steak pie, large gammon steaks, local beef, lasagne, spicy bean casserole and an ever-changing specials board.

Family facilities
Children are welcome indoors.

☛ Where to go from here
Take a look around Broughton-in-Furness, a pleasant village near the Duddon Estuary. Chestnut trees surround the village square, where there is an obelisk erected to commemorate the jubilee of George III, and a set of stocks. Broughton's oldest building is the Church of St Mary Magdalene, which has Saxon walls and a Norman archway.

Meandering in Newlands

A classic Lakeland cycle route in Newlands Valley, west of Derwent Water.

Newlands Valley

Tiny Newlands Church is whitewashed on the outside and white painted within, making it a light and airy place as well as one of great peace. It was rebuilt in 1843 on the site of an earlier church, and has a 17th-century pulpit and communion table. It is unusual among English parish churches in having no dedication to a particular saint. It stands close to the hamlet of Little Town, which is said to have inspired children's author Beatrix Potter to set there the story of Mrs Tiggywinkle, the hedgehog washerwoman.

The ride gives great fell views, but glimpses of only one lake – Bassenthwaite, to the north. And here's a good pub quiz question: how many lakes are there in the Lake District? Based on names, the answer is just one – Bassenthwaite Lake. All the rest are 'meres' or 'waters'. Bassenthwaite has recently gained new prominence as the site chosen by the first ospreys to nest in England since 1840. They arrived at Bassenthwaite in 2001, an event that gave the district a huge boost in the wake of the dreadful foot-and-mouth epidemic which devastated the area in that year.

the ride

1 From the parking place head up the steep hill to **Little Town**. Once through Little Town, relax and enjoy a fine winding, mostly downhill, run through the valley to **Stair** and a junction at the bottom of a hill.

2 Turn sharp right on to a narrow lane. The sign, half-hidden by vegetation, says 'Skelgill – Narrow Gated Road'. Climb again, not too steeply, with the hill of **Cat Bells** ahead. The lane steepens as it twists through the tiny hamlet of **Skelgill**, reaching a gate just above. The gate forces a stop,

and it is the top of the climb, so a good place for a look around. To the left of the isolated **Swinside Hill**, to the north, the stretch of water you can see is **Bassenthwaite Lake**. The lane passes a small parking area before reaching a T-junction on a bend. Turn left, downhill, over a cattle-grid and round another sharp bend. There'll usually be lots of parked cars here as it's the start of the main route up Cat Bells. The road levels out, then climbs to a junction.

3 Go left; the junction proves to be triangular. Go left again. As the road swings round to the right there are great views up the valley and the surrounding fells: **Maiden Moor, Dale Head, Hindscarth** and **Robinson**. Just beyond is the **Swinside Inn**. Turn right beside the pub on a narrow lane signed to Ullock and Braithwaite. Keep left where a road branches off right to Ullock.

4 Cross a stone-arched bridge over **Newlands Beck** and begin a short climb, steep at the start. As it levels out there's another fleeting glimpse of **Bassenthwaite Lake**. At a T-junction turn sharp left. The road runs south, generally level along the base of the steep slopes, and just high enough above the valley floor to give open views. Dip down to a small bridge. Just beyond is the start of the principal walkers' path up **Causey Pike**; you may well see figures struggling up the initial steep slope of **Rowling End**. A little further on, keep straight on past a sharp left turn (for Stair, Portinscale and Grange). For a little while the views are blocked by trees, mostly

Farmhouses in Newlands Vale

— 1h15 — 7 MILES — 11.3 KM — LEVEL 1 2 —

MAP: OS Explorer OL 4 The English Lakes (NW)

START/FINISH: near Little Town, south of Skelgill; grid ref: NY 232194

TRAILS/TRACKS: lanes, mostly quiet

LANDSCAPE: gentle part-wooded valley surrounded by rugged fells

PUBLIC TOILETS: none on route

TOURIST INFORMATION: Keswick, tel 017687 72645

CYCLE HIRE: Keswick Mountain Bikes, tel 017687 75202; Grin Up North, Cockermouth, tel 01900 829600

THE PUB: Swinside Inn, Newlands, see Point **3** on route

🛈 Some ups and down but not too severe. Suitability: children 8+

Getting to the start

Little Town is a hamlet between Buttermere and Derwent Water, on a narrow lane 4 miles (6.4km) south of Braithwaite. Roadside parking is at the bottom of the hill, just south west of Little Town.

Why do this cycle ride?

Though close to Keswick's bustle, the Newlands valley lacks any major visitor attractions. As a happy result, rather like the Duddon valley in the south, it still feels like the Lake District is supposed to. It's still a place where farming matters as much as fell walking and where visitors can slip back into an easier pace of life. It is also surrounded by scenery that, even by Lakeland standards, is stunning. This is a Lake District cycling route par excellence; of course that means a few hills, but most of the going is easy.

Researched and written by: Jon Sparks

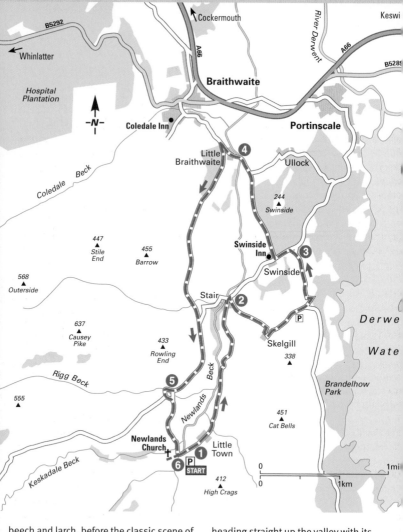

beech and larch, before the classic scene of the dale head begins to open up.

5 Very shortly, a steep stony track drops off to the left to a ford. Those seeking a moment's mountain-bike excitement can choose this track – it merely cuts off a short corner of the road. More sedately, continue round over a bridge to a **wooden house**. Turn left (signed to Newlands Church, Little Town) and drop down, then swing round,

heading straight up the valley with its glorious range of fells ahead.

6 As you come right down into the valley bottom, turn right on the no-through road to **Newlands Church** – closer even than the advertised 0.25 mile (400m). Retrace to the last junction and turn right, where it's only a few more pedal strokes to the bridge and the **car park** just beyond.

Swinside Inn

Situated in the peaceful Newlands valley, a world away from the hustle and bustle of Keswick, the Swinside Inn is a listed building dating back to about 1642. From the pub there are stunning views of Causey Pike and Cat Bells – among other landmarks. Although it's been modernised over the years, the two rustic and rambling bars retain many original features, including head-cracking low oak beams, winter log fires and a fine traditional black oak dresser in one of the bars. Good wholesome food, comfortable en suite bedrooms and a patio garden with memorable Lakeland views.

about the pub

Swinside Inn
Newlands, Keswick
Cumbria CA12 5UE
Tel 01687 78253
www.theswinsideinn.com

DIRECTIONS: 2.25 miles (3.6km) south west of Portinscale on a minor road signed to Newlands

PARKING: 50

OPEN: daily, all day

FOOD: daily

BREWERY/COMPANY: Scottish & Newcastle

REAL ALE: Theakston Best, Jennings Cumberland Ale, guest beer

ROOMS: 7 en suite

Food
The lunchtime menu is well adapted to hungry cyclists and walkers, with soup, sandwiches, ploughman's and a selection of cooked meals including home-made pies (steak, or chicken, mushroom and sage). The evening menu retains the pies and traditional pub favourites, alongside locally caught trout or Swinside chicken.

Family facilities
Children are welcome in the bars and overnight. There's a children's menu and older children can order small portions of main menu dishes. Safe garden.

Alternative refreshment stops
None on route. Pubs and cafés in Braithwaite (near Point 4) and in Keswick.

☛ Where to go from here
Whinlatter Forest is England's only true mountain forest. Visit the Osprey viewpoint at Dodd Wood and the Osprey exhibition at Whinlatter (www.ospreywatch.co.uk).

CYCLE

Newlands CUMBRIA

From Stonethwaite to Rosthwaite via Watendlath

With Walpole's 'Rogue' Herries by Dock Tarn and Watendlath.

The Herries family saga

One stormy night in 1739, Francis 'Rogue' Herries brought his family to live in the house his grandfather had built in Borrowdale. His son, David, 'woke again to see that all the horses were at a standstill and were gathered about a small stone bridge.' The 'hamlet...clustered beyond the bridge' was probably Grange. From there they crossed over a hill to come at last 'into a little valley, as still as a man's hand and bleached under the moon, but guarded by a ring of mountains that seemed to David gigantic.' This is the village of Rosthwaite, and the Hazel Bank

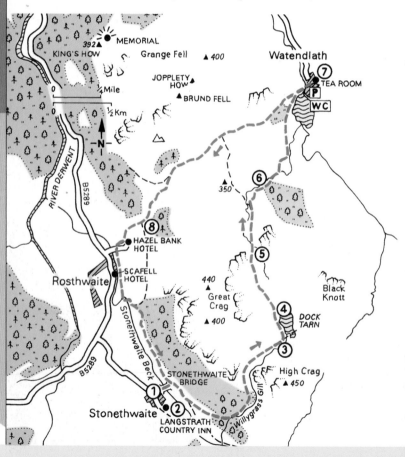

hotel sits on the spot where the Herries house stood. However, this house never existed except in the imagination of the novelist Hugh Walpole (1884–1941) and between the covers of the four volume series he wrote, collectively known as *The Herries Chronicle* (1930–33).

Walpole, one of the best-selling writers of his day, wrote over 50 novels. He bought a house above Derwent Water in 1923 and two years later announced that he was 'pinning all my hopes on two or three Lakes' novels, which will at least do something for this adorable place'. What he eventually produced over a five year period was a romantic history of a Lake District family from 1730 to 1932. Woven into the Herries' story are the major historic events of the period. The Jacobite Rebellion of 1745 passes near by in Carlisle, 'Rogue' Herries' son David dies at Uldale as the Bastille falls in 1789 and Judith, David's daughter, gives birth to her son, Adam, in Paris as Napoleon is finally defeated in 1815.

'Rogue' Herries, soon notorious in Borrowdale for his wildness, completes his infamy by selling his mistress at a fair. His consuming, unrequited love for Mirabell Starr, a gypsy woman, drives him to wander the country in search of her.

the walk

1 Walk down the track from the right-angled bend in the road just below the phone box and postbox in **Stonethwaite**. Cross **Stonethwaite Bridge** and go through a gate, then turn right on to the bridleway to

Stone footbridge across Watendlath Beck

3h30 **4.5 MILES** **7.2 KM** **LEVEL 1 2 3**

WALK

Stonethwaite CUMBRIA

MAP: OS Explorer OL 4 The English Lakes (NW)

START/FINISH: by phone-box in Stonethwaite; grid ref: NY 262137

PATHS: bridleways, fairly good paths and some rough walking

LANDSCAPE: fells, forest, tarns and lakes

PUBLIC TOILETS: Watendlath

TOURIST INFORMATION: Keswick, tel 017687 72645

THE PUB: Langstrath Country Inn, Stonethwaite, see Point **2** on route

🛑 Steep ascent in early stages, steep eroded descent later. Suitability: children 10+

Getting to the start

Stonethwaite lies south of Derwent Water and Rosthwaite village, off the B5289. There is limited parking near the phone-box in the village. If all spaces are taken retrace up the lane to wide verges at the edge of the village.

Researched and written by:
Moira McCrossan, Jon Sparks, Hugh Taylor

WALK

Grasmere. Go through another gate and after about 300yds (274m), just after a slight descent, look for a path off to the left, through a gap in the low wall. This is opposite the campsite across the valley.

2 Follow this path uphill and cross a stile into a wood. Above a second stile the path climbs in steep, unrelenting zigzags through the trees. The path emerges from the trees, still climbing, with spectacular views back to **Eagle Crag**. Cross another stile and keep following the path, now more level, bearing slightly right, until **Dock Tarn** appears.

3 Follow the obvious path around the left side of the tarn. There are some rocky sections but the going isn't too difficult. If the lower path is flooded, there are higher paths available to your left that lead in the same direction.

4 Passing a tiny pebble beach at the north end of the tarn, the path continues on the same heading, keeping right of a prominent rocky knoll. A view opens up ahead with **Ether Knott** in the foreground and the shapely profile of **Skiddaw** beyond. Just past a small rock pinnacle on the left, **Watendlath** comes into view and the path descends a steep rocky staircase to a kissing gate.

Ducks enjoying the bright blue waters of Watendlath Tarn

5 Go through the gate, cross the beck and follow the green-topped **wooden posts** on a stone path across the bog. Turn right at a junction signposted 'Watendlath' and descend parallel to the wall until you can cross it at a kissing gate.

6 Follow the **stream** downhill, cross it, then follow the line of the wall down and left, funnelling into a walled track. Follow this to meet another track, bear right and then turn right across the old pack bridge into **Watendlath**.

7 From Watendlath recross the little bridge and follow the public bridleway sign to **Rosthwaite**. Walk uphill on this well-used route, cross a broad saddle, then go through a kissing gate and head downhill, passing a gate on the right. At the bottom of the hill a **broken slate slab** on the wall indicates that the path continues to Stonethwaite.

8 Ignore the sign and instead turn right through the gate in the wall, go downhill and pass through another gate. Cross the lane leading to the **Hazel Bank Hotel** and continue on a narrow path (bridleway sign) and follow this back to **Stonethwaite Bridge**.

Langstrath Country Inn

Even by Lake District standards, the setting of the Langstrath Country Inn is idyllic. At the end of the road in this little branch valley, there's hardly any traffic to disturb the tranquillity of the beer garden in the shade of a fine sycamore tree. Here you can savour the lovely views down the Stonethwaite valley to the commanding bulk of Eagle Crag, an unmistakable sight with its vertical edge. With Eagle Crag and other notable climbing crags in sight of the pub, it's especially appropriate that Jennings Crag Rat is among the real ales usually available: 'crag rat' is an affectionately mocking local term for rock-climber. The pub, an extended former miner's cottage of 1590, is a cosy place, especially in winter when a log fire warms the bar. With its setting at the heart of the fells and right on the route of the Coast-to-Coast Walk, it's no wonder that talk in the bar usually revolves around walking and climbing.

Food

Expect standard pub fare, including sandwiches and hearty soups, supplemented by more imaginative daily specials such as duck and wild boar pie.

about the pub

Langstrath Country Inn
Stonethwaite, Borrowdale
Keswick, Cumbria CA12 8SX
Tel 017687 77239

DIRECTIONS: just south of the bridge in the centre of Stonethwaite
PARKING: 20
OPEN: daily, all day; closed Sunday evening
FOOD: daily
BREWERY/COMPANY: free house
REAL ALE: Black Sheep Bitter, Coniston Bluebird, guest beers
DOGS: welcome in the garden only
ROOMS: 10 bedrooms

Family facilities

Children are welcome indoors during the day only, and there's no specific menu or facilities for them. However, the peaceful garden and stunning views should more than make up for this in summer.

Alternative refreshment stops

The Scafell Hotel at Rosthwaite and the tea room at Watendlath, where, on a fine day, you can eat outside.

☛ Where to go from here

The single track road to Watendlath from the Keswick to Borrowdale road is one of the most scenic in the Lake District. Half-way up you'll cross Ashness Bridge, with the much pictured backdrop of distant lakes and mountains. Also worth seeing are the spectacular Lodore Falls, the subject of Robert Southey's famous poem 'The Cataract of Lodore' (1820). You'll find the falls just behind the Hilton Lodore hotel.

From Keswick to Threlkeld

A linear ride along an old railway, with an optional return via Lakeland's greatest ancient site.

The Greta Valley

The railway to Keswick was completed in 1864, having taken just 18 months to build, at a total cost of £267,000 for 31 miles (50km), and with 135 bridges. Goods traffic declined quite early in its life. Passenger numbers peaked in 1913 at 182,000, but never really recovered after World War One, though the line struggled on until it finally closed in 1972.

The railway route passes the bobbin mill site at Low Briery. The Lake District once produced half of all the wooden

Castlerigg Stone Circle in winter

bobbins used by the world's textile industry, and Low Briery alone exported 40 million of these every year.

Whether you cycle there, drive there or take the bus, Castlerigg Stone Circle is a 'must-see' site. It may not be the most impressive such circle in Britain, but it's hard to think of one that has a finer location. Best of all, come early in the morning or late in the evening when there are few others around and your imagination can have free rein. It was probably built around 3000 BC, and no one today knows exactly what it was for, although significant astronomical alignments have been identified.

the ride

1 Ride down towards the **Leisure Centre** and bear left, signed Keswick Railway Footpath, past the former railway station, now a smart hotel. The old trackbed leads

1h30 — **9 MILES** — **14.5 KM** — **LEVEL 1 2 3**

SHORTER ALTERNATIVE ROUTE

1h00 — **8 MILES** — **12.9 KM** — **LEVEL 1 2 3**

MAP: OS Explorer OL 4 The English Lakes (NW) and OL 5 The English Lakes (NE)

START/FINISH: Keswick Leisure Centre; grid ref: NY 269238

TRAILS/TRACKS: old railway track, short section of cycle track beside main road, minor road; optional return on minor roads with short section of busy A road (or walk down pavement alongside)

LANDSCAPE: woodland and river valley; open farmland with views to fells on return via stone circle

PUBLIC TOILETS: Keswick

TOURIST INFORMATION: Keswick, tel 017687 72645

CYCLE HIRE: Keswick Mountain Bikes, Keswick, tel 017687 75202

THE PUB: Horse & Farrier Inn, Threlkeld, see Point **3** on route

🚲 Railway path section suitable for all ages. If continuing into Threlkeld, suitability: children 6+; if returning via stone circle, suitability: children 10+

Getting to the start

Follow the A66 to a roundabout north west of Keswick. Take the A5271 towards the town. After 300yds (274m) turn left , sign-posted 'Leisure Pool' and roadside parking.

Why do this cycle ride?

This route crosses and recrosses the river, running through woodland. Return the same way take the climb to Castlerigg Stone Circle.

Researched and written by: Jon Sparks

on to a bridge over the river and then over the **A5271**. Pass a housing estate on the left, then climb – more steeply than you'd expect from a railway track (the route here was disrupted by the construction of the A66 bypass and bridge). There's a **National Cycle Network/C2C sign** just before the route goes under **Greta Bridge**. At the end of an unusual elevated boardwalk section, look right and you can just see the top of a stone arch, once the mouth of a tunnel, indicating the original line of the railway. Continue with views of the river then past the caravans of **Low Briery**. Go under a bridge and pass an information board about the former **bobbin mill**.

2 Continue across a bridge over the **River Greta**, seemingly a simple flat span but actually supported by an inverted ironwork arch. There's a second, similar bridge, and then a third with its arch 'right side up'. Just

CYCLE

Keswick

CUMBRIA

before the fourth bridge an **old railway hut** is now a shelter and information point. The bridge overlooks the junction of the river with **Glenderaterra Beck**. Cross another inverted bridge, then go through a short **tunnel** (no need for lights). There's another bridge, another information shelter and then a cutting. Cross another bridge and make a short climb, where the original line of the railway has again been obliterated by the **A66**. Emerge alongside the busy road on a separate cycle track. After about 200yds (183m) swing left on the minor road to **Threlkeld**, and follow it into the village, past the church, to the **Horse and Farrier**.

3 Retrace the route as far as the last bridge you crossed, and go over. (You can, of course, return all the way along the railway track from this point.)

4 About 30yds (27m) past the bridge, turn sharp left through a small gate. A steep

drop down and a bumpy path take you under the A66 and soon lead out to a road. Turn right and climb, with good views of **St John's in the Vale** and **Helvellyn**. Make a sweeping descent and turn left just before it levels out.

5 Swing round through a little valley, then turn left again and climb steadily, now looking down the **Naddle Valley**. The climb is quite long, levelling out just as the **stone circle** appears in a field on the left. Almost at once the road sweeps down again. Drop down to a T-junction on the outskirts of **Keswick**.

6 Families may feel safer walking the next short section. Follow the road left to another T-junction, then turn right down the hill. Round the first bend and just before a **bridge** with slate parapets go left round a barrier onto a gravel path leading down onto the **railway track** and so back to the start.

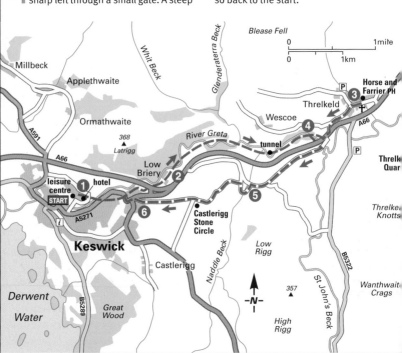

Horse & Farrier Inn

For over 300 years this stone inn has stood in an idyllic position below Blencathra. Ever popular with fell walkers, it provides imaginative home cooking, and real ales from the host brewer, Jennings. It has recently been refurbished, but original features have been retained and restored to their former glory, including slate floors, some fine panelling and oak beams. Hunting prints hang on the walls and warming log fires burn in the grate to create a cosy, welcoming atmosphere. It is noted locally for imaginative, rather restaurany food, although there is plenty of space for drinkers, and walkers are welcome in the bar. Garden seating has views up to the scarred face of Blencathra.

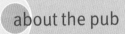

about the pub

Horse & Farrier Inn

Threlkeld, Keswick
Cumbria CA12 4SQ
Tel 017687 79688
www.horseandfarrier.com

DIRECTIONS: on the village main street, east of the church

PARKING: 60

OPEN: daily, all day

FOOD: daily, all day in summer

BREWERY/COMPANY: Jennings Brewery

REAL ALE: Jennings Bitter, Cocker Hoop and Sneck Lifter, guest beer

ROOMS: 9 en suite

Food

An adventurous menu offers plenty of choice including fresh fish and local produce. Starters like stir-fried king prawns and giant mussels with green chillies, and smoked haddock and sea trout terrine might precede fillet of red mullet with egg noodles and a Thai green curry sauce or pan-fried venison steak in a juniper marinade. Additional lunchtime fare includes cold and hot open sandwiches, and seasonal salads.

Family facilities

Children are welcome in the bars and overnight. 'Lakeside Larry's' menu offers a standard selection of children's meals, and various puzzles and drawings to colour in.

Alternative refreshment stops

Excellent choice of pubs, cafés and restaurants in Keswick and the Salutation pub in Threlkeld.

☞ Where to go from here

The Cars of the Stars Motor Museum in Keswick houses an unusual collection of cars from film and TV, including Chitty Chitty Bang Bang, the Batmobile and the James Bond cars. North of Keswick on the A591 is Mirehouse, a 17th-century house in a spectacular lakeside setting, near where Tennyson wrote much of *Morte d'Arthur*.

Keswick's Walla Crag above Derwent Water

Keswick

CUMBRIA

Wonderful panoramas to the surrounding fells, a jewelled lake and sylvan splendour are the delights of this walk.

Derwent Water and Walla Crag

At the foot of Borrowdale – often referred to as the most beautiful valley in England – the northern head of Derwent Water opens to Keswick and the northern fells with dramatic effect. The highlight of this walk is undeniably the staggering view from the heights of Walla Crag. West across Derwent Water, beyond Cat Bells, Maiden Moor and the secretive Newland Valley stand the striking north western fells of Causey Pike, Sail, Crag Hill and Grisedale Pike. To the south west rise Glaramara and Great Gable. To the north, Skiddaw and Blencathra.

The lake is 3 miles (4.8km) long and 72ft (22m) deep and is fed by the River Derwent. A speed limit ensures that motor-powered boats do not ply its waters. Seasonal salmon, brown trout, Arctic char, perch and the predatory pike swim beneath the surface. There are four islands on the lake, all owned by the National Trust. The

largest and most northerly of the four is Derwent Isle. Once owned by Fountains Abbey it was bought by German miners from the Company of Mines Royal in 1569. The island and part of its grand 18th-century house are open to visitors on a handful of days during the year. St Herbert's Island was reputedly home to a Christian missionary in the 10th century, and monks remained in residence after his departure. A ruined summer house is all that stands there today. By the path, just above Derwent Bay, is an inscribed slate plaque in honour of Canon H D Rawnsley who did much to keep the lake as it remains today. He was vicar of Crosthwaite, the parish church of Keswick, from 1883 to 1917, and was one of Lakeland's greatest conservationists. In 1895 he became a co-founder of the National Trust. He was a campaigner against rude postcards and also encouraged children's author Beatrix Potter to publish her first book, *The Tale of Peter Rabbit*, in 1900.

Top: Small boats between wooden jetties, seen from Friars Crag on the edge of Derwent Water
Right: Friars Crag across Derwent Water

the walk

WALK

1 Proceed down the road to **Derwent Bay**. Go left opposite the landing stages, past a toilet block, on the track through **Cockshot Wood**. At a fork take the higher left-hand path. Exit the wood on to a fenced path across a field to the **Borrowdale road**. Cross, and climb stone steps into **Castlehead Wood**. Turn left, then bear right and climb steeply, levelling off at a shoulder. In a little way a steeper path climbs to the right, to **Castle Head**'s rocky summit – a great viewpoint.

2 Return to the shoulder, then turn right, downhill, curving right but keeping left at a fork, until rough steps lead down to a kissing gate. Take a path between fields to a road and houses. Go right and follow the road to its end at **Springs Farm**. Bear left on a track climbing through **Springs Wood**. Bear right at a fork, then follow the edge of the wood, passing a **TV mast**. At a kissing gate, dip back into the wood, cross a footbridge and go up rough steps to a lane. Turn right and follow the lane to its end below **Rakefoot**.

3 Cross the footbridge and ascend the rough track by the stone wall. Go through a gate to open fell and follow the wall up right. At a dip the main path cuts off the corner of the wall and rises to a kissing gate. The path beyond this runs close to steep, unfenced drops in places. (To avoid these simply follow the wall left to a stile near the summit cairn.) Follow the path, crossing the head of a gully (**Lady's Rake**), and climb to the polished rock cap of **Walla Crag** and superb views.

PATHS: OS Explorer OL 4 The English Lakes (NW)

START/FINISH: Lakeside car park, Keswick; grid ref: NY 265229

PATHS: good paths and tracks, steep ascent and descent, 3 stiles

LANDSCAPE: woods, open fell and lakeside

PUBLIC TOILETS: at the car park and above the landing stages

TOURIST INFORMATION: Keswick, tel 017687 72645

THE PUB: Lake Road Inn, Keswick, near start of route

🅵 Paths run close to steep, unfenced drops on Walla Crag (an alternative route avoiding these is suggested). Suitability: children 10+, avoiding route 7+

Getting to the start

From central Keswick, take the B5289 Borrowdale road at the western end of the town. Follow it for 600yds (549m) and turn right to reach the Lakeside car park.

Researched and written by:
Bill Birkett, Jon Sparks

Keswick CUMBRIA

Keswick CUMBRIA

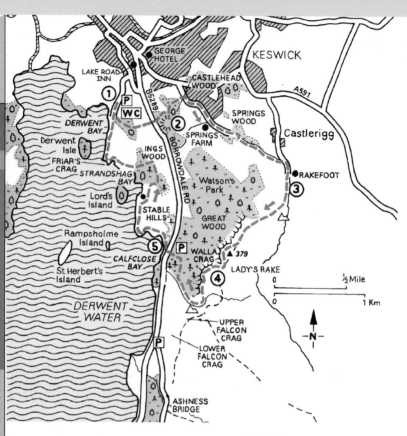

4 Continue in the same line to a stile and
cross back over the wall. A grassy path
descends parallel to the wall, becoming
steeper as it drops towards **Cat Gill**. Keep
descending steeply, with stone steps and
slippery rock, until a track bears right near
a footbridge, descending more easily
through **Great Wood**. At a junction of
tracks, drop down left to a tarmac track
and straight across down a path to a gap
in the wall by the **Borrowdale road**. Another
gap in the wall opposite and a short path
lead to the **lake shore**.

what to look for

The rocky knoll of Friar's Crag,
with its stand of Scots pine, is one of
the most famous lakeside viewpoints. It is said to
take its name from the monks who once lived on
St Herbert's Island. At the foot of the crag,
attached to the rocks which are often submerged
when the lake level is high, memorial plaques
detail all the former mayors of Keswick.

5 Go right, following the shore around
Calfclose Bay. Leave the shore to skirt
round **Stable Hills**, following its drive until a
gate on the left leads to a path through

damp **Ings Wood**. The path continues
round **Strandshag Bay** to **Friar's Crag**. Go
right and easily back via **Derwent Bay** to
the **car park**.

Lake Road Inn

There's a bewildering choice of pubs in Keswick, most of them serving decent beer and regular pub food. But if you walk up from the Lakeside car park and through the little underpass, one of the first pubs you come to is the Lake Road Inn, and it turns out to be a good choice. The interior has some fine panelling and comfortable seating, giving it a cosy feel that's matched by one of the friendliest welcomes in the district. It also serves its range of robust, well-priced food throughout the day, which is important where walkers and climbers are concerned.

Food
From the printed menu you can choose filled jacket potatoes, roast ham salad, Cumberland sausage and onion baguettes, and main courses such as steak pie, lasagne, chilli, and chicken Kiev. Puddings include sticky toffee pudding with ice cream.

Family facilities
Families are welcome indoors and young children have a selection of standard children's meals to choose from. Enclosed patio garden away from the road.

Alternative refreshment stops
There are cafés and tea-gardens in Keswick near the start of the walk.

☛ Where to go from here
The Derwentwater Motor Launch Company runs regular sailings both clockwise and anticlockwise around the lake. Landing stages en route include Ashness Gate, Lodore, High Brandlehow, Low Brandlehow, Hawes End and Nichol End. It makes for a good walk to take the boat out and return by foot to Keswick. Family tickets offer good value.

Boats moored at Derwent Water

about the pub

Lake Road Inn

Lake Road, Keswick
Cumbria CA12 5BT
Tel 017687 72404

DIRECTIONS: near the Lakeside car park
PARKING: use town car parks
OPEN: daily, all day
FOOD: daily, all day
BREWERY/COMPANY: Jennings Brewery
REAL ALE: full range of Jennings beers
DOGS: welcome in the old barn and garden only

Coniston CUMBRIA

From Coniston to Tarn Hows

Explore the wooded intricacies of Yewdale before reaching the scenic favourite of Tarn Hows.

Coniston

This long route of great variety, much interest and heart-stopping beauty contrasts the quiet mixed woods in and around the fringes of forgotten Yewdale, with the popular Tarn Hows, and views back over Coniston Water or west to the mountains of Coniston Old Man and Wetherlam.

Copper mining started in the bowels of the mountain, Coniston Old Man, during the Bronze Age. So extensive were these early workings that when a group of German miners, brought over in Elizabethan times to kickstart 'modern mineral mining' in Britain, started work, they were shocked to find that the mountain was already riddled with workings. They referred to these earlier sites as 'the old men workings', which is possibly one derivation of the modern name Coniston Old Man.

Coniston Water is some 5 miles (8km) long and reaches a maximum depth of 184ft (56m). It is the third largest of the Lakeland lakes. It once provided an important fish source for the monks of Furness Abbey, who owned the lake and much of the surrounding land in the 13th and 14th centuries. Many of their iron bloomery and charcoal burning sites remain intact around the shores of the lake. The copper mines were revitalised around 1859, and at the height of production some 800 men worked in Coppermines Valley above the village.

Speed ace Donald Campbell was killed on Coniston Water in 1967, attempting to beat his own water speed record. His boat became airborne and crashed, but in 2001 was raised from the bed of the lake. He is buried in St Andrew's Church.

the walk

1 Exit the **car park** on to the main road (**Tilberthwaite Avenue**) and turn right. In a few hundred paces a road leads off left, signposted to Ambleside. Follow this beyond the football field to a stone bridge on the right, over **Yewdale Beck**. Cross and go immediately left over the low stone stile. Go through a kissing gate into a field. Follow the path curving right and gently uphill beside a stone wall. The path leads to a recently renovated **stone building**.

3h30 · **6.75 MILES** · **10.9 KM** · **LEVEL 2**

PATHS: OS Explorer OL 7 The English Lakes (SE)

START/FINISH: Coniston car park; grid ref: SD 303975

PATHS: road, grassy paths and tracks, 4 stiles

LANDSCAPE: woods, field, fell, tarn and lake

PUBLIC TOILETS: at car park

TOURIST INFORMATION: Ambleside, tel 015394 32582

THE PUB: Black Bull Inn, Coniston, see Point **1** on route

🔵 Suitability: children 8+

Getting to the start

Coniston is just off the B593 between Broughton-in-Furness and Ambleside. Approaching from Ambleside, go down the short main street and turn left just after the Black Bull Inn, before the bridge. The main car park is obvious, on the right, a short way past the church.

Researched and written by: Bill Birkett, Jon Sparks

Tourists on a trip across Coniston Water

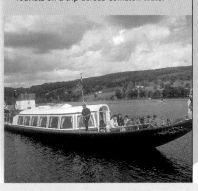

5 Turn right immediately before the dam and descend the path to the right of the beck. This is steep and rocky in places. At the bottom go left over the footbridge, then out on to the **Coniston road**. Cross and go left. Turn right towards **Yewtree Farm** and right again before the farmyard. Follow the track up to another gate, then go left above the fence. Keep along this grassy track, ignoring branches to the right, to pass above **High Yewdale Farm**. A final gate leads out to a narrow road. Turn left over **Shepherd's Bridge** and meet the **Coniston road**.

6 Cross and go left until, opposite **High Yewdale Farm**, a path leads right along a line of yew trees. Around 200yds (183m) beyond the last of the trees, bear right across the fields and straight ahead through the farmyard of **Low Yewdale**. Go left along a track, over a bridge, and continue alongside the beck. The track curves away from the stream. At a sharp bend go right, signposted 'Cumbria Way', through the field. Beyond a wall the track is indistinct: keep parallel to the walled wood on the left. The track becomes clear again and enters **Back Guards Plantation**. Follow the track through the wood. Pass through yew trees and descend to join the outward route back into **Coniston village**.

2 Pass the building on the left and ascend through a gate. Go up a little further, then take a branch path right below the mass of gorse. Go up to a little gate through the stone wall enclosing **High Guards Wood**. Climb steeply through the Scots pine. Cross a ruined stone wall and follow the waymarked path to descend through **Guards Wood**. Leave the wood and continue down a stony track, muddy in places, to a gate and stile leading on to a **stony lane**.

3 Go left up the lane. In a few hundred paces go right through a gate. Follow the track winding up through fields, through one gate and then a gate/stile. The grassy track meets a fence beside **Tarn Hows Wood**. Keep right along the track and continue to a steep, surfaced track. **Tarn Hows Cottage** is below to the left. Go right along the track to a road. Go left, ascending the road and passing a **car park**. Take the track opposite the car park entrance, then bear off right, across the slope overlooking **Tarn Hows**.

4 Several tracks come together to form one clear track. Follow this to make an anticlockwise circuit of the tarn. At the end of the circuit is a little **dam**.

what to look for

The Victorian philosopher and art critic John Ruskin lived at Brantwood, across the lake, from 1871 until 1901. He was buried at St Andrew's Church in Coniston. His grave is marked with a large cross carved from local green slate. Designed by his secretary, Lakeland authority W G Collingwood, it depicts aspects of Ruskin's work and life.

Black Bull Inn

The Black Bull sits just above Church Beck and in the shadow of the Old Man, and has been at the heart of Coniston village for nearly 400 years. Walls in the black-beamed bar are adorned with many photos celebrating the history of the village and the pub, and in particular the late Donald Campbell, who stayed here while preparing for the attempt on the world water speed record which cost him his life. Both the painter J M W Turner and the poet Samuel Taylor Coleridge also enjoyed the hospitality of this old coaching inn. The Coniston Brewery behind the pub supplies the beer, so sample a pint of Bluebird and see just why it won the title Champion Beer of Britain.

Food
The wide-ranging menu caters for all tastes, from sandwiches, ploughman's lunches and salads to freshly battered haddock and chips, local Esthwaite trout, half a shoulder of local lamb and generous Cumbrian grills. Separate evening restaurant menu.

about the pub

Black Bull Inn
1 Yewdale Road, Coniston
Cumbria LA21 8DU
Tel 015394 41335
www.conistonbrewery.com

DIRECTIONS: just west of St Andrew's Church in Coniston	
PARKING: 12	
OPEN: daily, all day	
FOOD: daily, all day	
BREWERY/COMPANY: free house	
REAL ALE: Coniston Bluebird, XB, Old Man – all brewed at the pub	
DOGS: welcome in the the pub	
ROOMS: 15 en suite	

Family facilities
The pub has a children's licence, so kids are welcome throughout the pub and young children have their own menu. Summer seating on the riverside patio.

Alternative refreshment stops
There is plenty of choice in Coniston. The Crown Inn also does bar meals, and there is a good café at Bridge End.

☛ Where to go from here
The restored steam yacht *Gondola*, built in 1859, was relaunched in 1980 and plies Coniston Water every summer. The trip starts at Coniston Pier, passing Coniston Hall and stopping at Brantwood, before returning.

Bardsea and Birkrigg Common

Bardsea

CUMBRIA

A circuit of the common to discover ancient remains.

Birkrigg Common

Birkrigg Common is an open expanse of bracken, grass and low limestone scars, rising between the shores of Morecambe Bay and the gentle valley containing Urswick Tarn. Although only a lowly height, it offers splendid views encompassing the whole of Morecambe Bay and most of the Furness Peninsula, with Black Combe and the Coniston fells prominently in view. Other Lakeland fell groups, the Yorkshire Dales and Bowland feature more distantly. The Common is criss-crossed with innumerable paths and can be explored at will, but the described walk gives a good introduction.

The bedrock of the common is carboniferous limestone, which outcrops only on the margins of the Lake District, most notably around Morecambe Bay and Kendal, but also around Shap and above Pooley Bridge. It was laid down in a shallow sea and once covered the whole of the Lake District, before the area was pushed up into a vast dome by earth movements. Subsequent erosion largely removed most of the limestone layer, exposing the volcanic core of the Lake District. Birkrigg Common is dry, as most limestone areas are. Not far away, however, water has pooled to form the lovely little reed-fringed Urswick Tarn, which is a haven for waterfowl. Some ground water contained in the limestone layer reaches the surface as freshwater springs out on the sands of Morecambe Bay.

The area around Birkrigg Common was always fairly dry and fertile, compared to the higher Lakeland fells, so it attracted the attention of early settlers. Little remains to be seen, but the most notable feature is a small early Bronze Age stone circle of limestone boulders on the seaward slopes. Several tumuli are dotted around, and a rumpled series of low, grassy earthworks represent the remains of an ancient homestead site. Above Great Urswick, a low hill encircled by a limestone scar bears a hill fort, probably dating from the Iron Age, in the centuries preceding the Roman conquest. Very little is known about these ancient settlement sites, but there has been a continual human presence in the area for over 4,000 years.

A view from Birkrigg Common across Morecambe Bay

the walk

1 Turn right along the shoreline to **Sea Wood**, where the main road veers away and trees come right down to the water's edge. Here you can either continue along the shore or follow a parallel path just inside the wood. If you follow the shore, keep a lookout for the end of the wood. (A line of trees continues along the shore but with fields above.) Scramble up into the wood, and follow a path up just inside its edge to the road. Cross to gain a broader verge and turn left up the road. As the road swings left, turn right at a gate into another part of **Sea Wood**.

2 Follow the path into the wood, keeping left at any forks, always close to the edge of the wood. Leave the wood at a gate on to a lane. Cross over and follow a grassy path through bracken on to **Birkrigg Common**, aiming for a wall corner and then keep straight ahead for another 100yds (91m) to a small **stone circle**. Follow any grassy path through the bracken to the

Looking across Birkrigg Common over Bardsea with the coast and sea behind

1h30 — 4 MILES — 6.4 KM — LEVEL 1 2 3

PATHS: OS Explorer OL 6 The English Lakes (SW); OL 7 The English Lakes (SE)

START/FINISH: small car parks between coast road and shore, Bardsea; grid ref: SD 301742 (on Explorer OL 7)

PATHS: paths and tracks, some field paths may be muddy

LANDSCAPE: low-lying, rolling limestone country, with coastal margin, woodland and open common

PUBLIC TOILETS: on coast road below Bardsea

TOURIST INFORMATION: Ulverston, tel 01229 587120

THE PUB: Braddylls Arms, Main Street, Bardsea, see Point **1** on route

 Suitability: all ages

Getting to the start

Bardsea is located on the A5087, 2.5 miles (4km) south of Ulverston and the A590. Park in any of the large lay-bys along the coastal road.

Researched and written by:
Paddy Dillon, Jon Sparks

Bardsea CUMBRIA

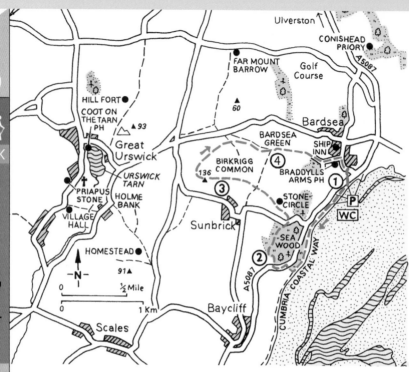

Ulverston ↑

CONISHEAD PRIORY

FAR MOUNT BARROW

Golf Course

A5087

HILL FORT ●

COOT ON THE TARN PH ▲ 93

Great Urswick

URSWICK TARN

PRIAPUS STONE

HOLME BANK

VILLAGE HALL

HOMESTEAD ●

91 ▲

–N–

0   ½ Mile

0   1 Km

Scales

Sunbrick

▲ 60

Bardsea

BARDSEA GREEN

SHIP INN

BIRKRIGG COMMON

136 ▲

④

BRADDYLLS ARMS PH ①

③

STONE CIRCLE

P

WC

②

SEA WOOD

A5087

CUMBRIA COASTAL WAY

Baycliff

high skyline. Birkrigg Common bears a **trig point** at 446ft (136m), and there are fine views from here.

3 At the trig point turn right along a broad, level, grassy band, which is aligned almost exactly on the **Barrow monument** on Ulverston's **Hoad Hill**. Follow this highway, bearing slightly right as it begins to descend, between bands of limestone and stands of gorse. As the

limestone peters out and gorse gives way to bracken, cross one green path across the hillside. At a second similar path, turn right. At a complex junction of tracks keep straight ahead on the most level track. As the path starts to descend, Bardsea appears ahead, and then a **wall** runs across in front of you.

4 Turn left on a path parallel to the wall and down into a corner of walls. Go right through a gate and follow a pleasant track downhill to a cluster of houses at **Bardsea Green**. The track becomes a tarmac road: follow this through a dip. Keep left at a junction and up into **Bardsea**, then right at the **Braddylls Arms** and follow a road down to the shore. Where this road forks you may want to go left or right depending on exactly where along the shoreline you started from.

what to look for

Sea Wood belonged to Lady Jane Grey, Queen of England for only nine days in 1554. It was held by the Crown until the 1950s and is now managed by the Woodland Trust. Information boards at the access points list the tree species, flora and fauna you'll find here.

Braddylls Arms

There's something special about the views over Morecambe Bay, with the play of light, the ebb and flow of the tides – and the longer-term shifts of channels and sandbanks means that they are never the same twice. A walk on Birkrigg Common, splendid though it is, will probably do no more than whet your appetite for this ever-changing panorama. The Braddylls Arms, a former coaching inn dating from the 16th century, is a perfect place to savour it a little longer. After recent restoration, the conservatory-style dining room offers this wonderful view to every table. The patio terraces outside, embellished with potted palms, give an even better view. While enjoying the views you can also quench your thirst with Black Sheep or Timothy Taylor's beers and tuck into a meal from an extensive menu.

about the pub

Braddylls Arms
Main Street, Bardsea
Ulverston, Cumbria LA12 9QT
Tel 01229 869707

DIRECTIONS:	to the south of the centre of Bardsea village
PARKING:	44
OPEN:	daily, all day Saturday & Sunday
FOOD:	daily
BREWERY/COMPANY:	free house
REAL ALE:	Black Sheep Bitter, Timothy Taylor Landlord
DOGS:	garden only
ROOMS:	4 en suite

Food

Light bites include a ploughman's lunch, a hot salad of chicken, bacon and avocado, and tagliatelle with Mediterranean sauce. For something more substantial order steak and kidney pie, lamb Henry with creamy mash, pork loin with mustard sauce, or one of the fresh fish specials.

Family facilities

Families will enjoy the patio and view on fine days. Children are welcome indoors and small children have their own menu.

☞ Where to go from here

Wander round the cobbled Market Street in nearby Ulverston. You'll find market stalls on Thursdays and Saturdays, and a world champion town crier. Conishead Priory, between Ulverston and Bardsea, is now a Buddhist study centre with a pleasant woodland trail.

From Elterwater to Loughrigg Tarn

Bluebell woods, a lake,
a tarn, a waterfall and
Little Loughrigg make
this a memorable outing.

Elter Water

The little lake of Elter Water and petite Loughrigg Tarn are amongst the prettiest stretches of water in Lakeland. The former, really three interconnected basins, was originally named Eltermere, which translates directly from the Old Norse (or Viking) into 'swan lake'. The swans are still here in abundance – be careful they don't grab your sandwiches should you choose to eat your lunch on the wooden bench at the foot of the lake. The views over both lake and tarn to the reclining lion profile of the Langdale Pikes are particularly evocative.

Each season paints a different picture here, with golden daffodils by Langdale Beck in early spring, bluebells in Rob Rash woods in May, yellow maple in Elterwater village in October and a thousand shades of green, everywhere, all summer. This is very much a walk for all seasons, and should the section through the meadows

what to look for

Carrying the full contents of the River Brathay over a vertical drop of some 30ft (9m), Skelwith Force waterfall is an impressive sight. A little bridge provides access to the rocks above the force, and steps and a walkway lead to lower rocks and a good viewpoint. Access is unrestricted, though the rocks are polished and the waterfall unguarded. A weir once diverted water from above the falls to power the mills at Skelwith Bridge just downstream.

At Skelwith Bridge, rock extracted from a quarry above Kirkstone Pass is sawn, split and polished. It has many uses, from practical roofing slates to decorative panels that clad prestige buildings, to ornamental coffee tables. Some of the finished products can be viewed in the Touchstone Interiors gallery just below the works to the right of the path.

by the Brathay be flooded, then a simple detour can easily be made on to the road to bypass the problem.

With all the quarrying and mining that once took place in the Lake District, there used to be a considerable demand for 'black powder', or gunpowder, as it is more commonly known. Without treason or plot, Elterwater Gunpowder works, founded in 1824, once filled that demand. The natural water power of Langdale Beck was utilised to drive great grinding wheels or millstones. Prime quality charcoal came from the local coppices, and saltpetre and sulphur were imported. In the 1890s the works employed

around 80 people. Accidental explosions did occur, notably in 1916 when four men were killed. The whole enterprise closed down in 1929. Today the site is occupied by the Langdale Timeshare organisation, with only the massive mill wheels on display to bear witness to times past.

the walk

1 Go through a small gate and walk downstream beside **Great Langdale Beck** and through the mixed woods of **Rob Rash**. A little gate leads through a stone wall, and the open foot of Elter Water lies to the right. Continue along the path through the meadows by the river. This section can be wet and is prone to flooding. Pass through a gate and enter mixed woods. Keep along the path to pass **Skelwith Force** waterfall down to the right. A bridge leads across a channel to a viewing point. Keep along the path to pass through industrial buildings belonging to **Kirkstone Quarry**.

2 Kirkstone Galleries (now called **Touchstone Interiors**) is on the right, as the path becomes a small surfaced road. Continue to meet the **A593** by the bridge, where there are picnic benches. Turn left to pass the **Skelwith Bridge hotel**. At the road junction, cross directly over the Great Langdale road to reach a lane just left of the phone-box and bus shelter. Follow the lane, steeply at first, to a T-junction. Turn right over the bridge, then bear left up a narrow path. Go left on a track and then fork right,

Left: Hikers at Elterwater
Right: Loughrigg Tarn

2h00 **4 MILES** **6.4 KM** **LEVEL 2**

PATHS: OS Explorer OL 7 The English Lakes (SE)
START/FINISH: National Trust pay-and-display car park, Elterwater; grid ref: NY 328048
PATHS: grassy and stony paths and tracks, surfaced lane, 4 stiles
LANDSCAPE: lake, tarn, fields, woods, open fellside, views to fells
PUBLIC TOILETS: above car park in Elterwater village
TOURIST INFORMATION: Ambleside, tel 015394 32582
THE PUB: The Britannia Inn, Elterwater, see Point **1** on route
🚶 Suitability: all ages

Getting to the start
Elterwater village lies about 5 miles (8km) west of Ambleside. At Skelwith Bridge turn on to the B5343 and soon bear left to reach the village. The main car park is on the left just before the bridge.

Researched and written by:
Bill Birkett, Jon Sparks

17
WALK
Elterwater CUMBRIA

81

in front of a row of **cottages**. Where the track splits, bear left, through a gate with a sign for **Loughrigg Tarn and Grasmere**. Follow the track to overlook the tarn. Half-way along the tarn cross the stile over the iron railings on the left.

3 Follow the footpath down the meadow to traverse right, just above the tarn. The path bears right to climb a **ladder stile** over a stone wall. Follow the grassy track up the hill to a gate and stile on to the road. Turn left along the road, until a surfaced drive leads up to the right, signposted **'Public Footpath Skelwith Bridge'**. Pass a small cottage. The track becomes much rougher as it passes a higher cottage, **Crag Head**. By a holly tree about 50yds

(46m) further on, a narrow path goes sharply back right, up the hillside, to gain a level shoulder between the craggy outcrops of **Little Loughrigg**.

4 Follow the path over the shoulder and past a little tarn on the right, then descend to meet a stone wall with railings on top. Follow the wall down, under power lines, and soon find a ladder stile leading over the wall into the upper woods of **Rob Rash**. A clear path descends steeply to the road. Cross diagonally right to a gap in the wall next to the large double gates. Descend a track to meet up with the outward route. Bear right to return to **Elterwater** village.

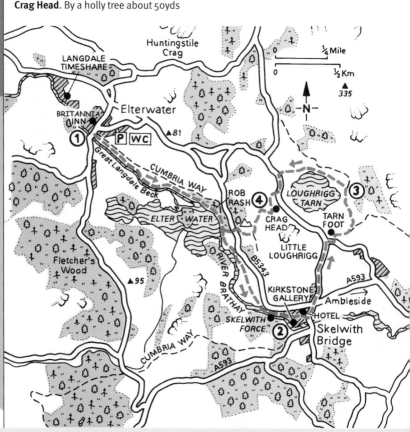

The Britannia Inn

Overlooking the village green in a famous scenic valley, The Britannia captures the essence of a traditional family-run Lakeland inn and has been a favourite with generations of walkers and climbers. It was originally a farmhouse and the premises of a local cobbler, and became a beer house in the 19th century. The Britannia really comes to life in summer when colourful hanging baskets dazzle the eye and the sunny terraced garden fills with walkers enjoying the fell views. In colder weather, real fires in the oak-beamed bar make the place snug and welcoming – the perfect place to retreat to at the end of a country walk. Add to all this some attractively furnished bedrooms, and The Britannia is an ideal base for a holiday or weekend break.

about the pub

The Britannia Inn
Elterwater, Ambleside
Cumbria LA22 9HP
Tel 015394 37210
www.britinn.net

DIRECTIONS: in the centre of the village
PARKING: limited – use walk car park
OPEN: daily, all day
FOOD: daily, all day
BREWERY/COMPANY: free house
REAL ALE: Jennings Bitter, Coniston Bluebird, Timothy Taylor Landlord, 2 guest beers
DOGS: welcome inside
ROOMS: 9 en suite

Food

Lunches, afternoon snacks and dinner are served daily. Hearty home-made snacks include warming soups, filled rolls, Herdwick lamb rogan josh, Cumberland sausage and mash, quiche, and steak and kidney pie. The more ambitious evening menu might offer steak Diane, fresh bream with red and yellow pepper sauces, or Lakeland lamb Henry.

Family facilities

On a fine day, families will find it a real pleasure to sit outside on the sunny tiered slate terraces looking over the village green and down the valley. There's a children's menu and usually a children's special too, and if you're there for afternoon tea, how about a 'Baa for Ewe' – sheep-shaped shortbread with chocolate chips.

Alternative refreshment stops

En route, Touchstone Interiors has a café, called Chesters, offering tea, coffee, cakes and light meals. The Skelwith Bridge Hotel also offers bar meals.

☛ Where to go from here

Charming Dove Cottage, at Grasmere, was a home of poet William Wordsworth and is now a museum to him (tel 015394 35544). From 1813 he lived at the grander Rydal Mount, near by, and designed the lovely gardens (tel 015394 33002).

St John's in the Vale from Legburthwaite

Exploring a compact valley and a wild fell.

St John's in the Vale

The walk visits the remote little church of St John's in the Vale. As you enter through the iron gate and archway of overhanging yew, the proportions of this slate-roofed, low, narrow stone building immediately seem just right. It's simple and unassuming, and with the parish history related on its assembled headstones it is a building in perfect harmony with its natural surroundings.

The quiet road which runs past the church was once of greater importance and linked communities on both sides of the high shoulder. There has long been a church on this site, and while the present building

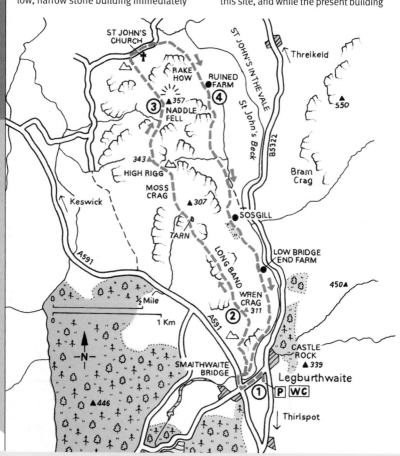

dates from 1845, headstones in the churchyard predate this considerably. It is thought that a reference in the chartulary of Fountains Abbey to 'dommus sancti Johannis' – a house of St John – may refer to a church here in the 13th century. The earliest definite reference to St John's is in 1554. The sundial is inscribed 'St John's Chapel, 1635' and a silver chalice (not kept within the church) was gifted in 1659. The registers within the church date from 1776 onwards.

With St John's in the Vale to the east and the Naddle Valley extension of the Thirlmere Valley to the west, Naddle Fell forms an attractive upland area which runs north from Thirlmere reservoir towards the great fells of Blencathra and Skiddaw. Its three tops – Wren Crag, High Rigg and Naddle Fell – straddle a shoulder of craggy outcrops, liberally sprinkled with a mix of bracken and ling heather. Tarnlets fill many of the hollows, rowan and Scots pine abound, and despite the presence of higher fells all around and roads occupying the dales below, this rugged fell has great charm and a surprising degree of isolation.

the walk

1 At the head of the car park a small gate leads on to the old road. Turn left and go down the lane to a gate that opens on to the verge of the busy **A591**. Turn right along this and cross **Smaithwaite Bridge** to a stile over the wall on the right. Cross the stile and take the path away from the road, soon swinging left and starting to climb. This leads through a stand of magnificent Scots pine, with fine views to **Castle Rock** across the dale, before a final rise to the open top of **Wren Crag**.

2h45 — **5 MILES** — **8 KM** — **LEVEL 1 2 3**

WALK

PATHS: OS Explorer OL 5 The English Lakes (NE)

START/FINISH: car park at Legburthwaite, head of St John's in the Vale; grid ref: NY 318195

PATHS: grassy paths and track, 8 stiles

LANDSCAPE: open fellside and river dale

PUBLIC TOILETS: at car park

TOURIST INFORMATION: Keswick, tel 017687 72645

THE PUB: The King's Head Hotel & Inn, Thirlspot, south of the route

🛈 Short section crosses steep slope above river. Suitability: children 6+

Getting to the start

Legburthwaite is a hamlet at the northern tip of Thirlmere, on the B5322. The car park area is under trees, 0.25 mile (400m) north of the junction with the A591.

Researched and written by: Bill Birkett, Jon Sparks

The perfect weather to sail a dinghy on Thirlmere reservoir

WALK

Legburthwaite CUMBRIA

2 Descend steeply into the dip and through the gap in the wall. Climb again to follow the crest of a line of rocky outcrops (**Long Band**). Drop down slightly, leftward, to a stile over a wire fence. Cross this, then go right, along the fence, to a little tarn in a hollow. Bear left, initially along a ruined wall, then down to a stile over a stone wall. Beyond the stile the path follows the wall, climbing to pass through a corridor formed by the rocky knoll of **Moss Crag**. As the corridor opens out, swing left, under the steep crag, then back right, skirting a marshy area. Climb a narrow path splitting the bracken to the top of **High Rigg**. Bear right and then back left along a high grassy ridge, above the pools of **Paper Moss**, to a hollow and pond. Ascend to the rocky summit of **Naddle Fell**, the highest point of this walk, with superb views to the high fells of **Blencathra** and **Skiddaw**.

3 A clear green path falls down the steepening hillside ahead. Skirt the buildings above **St John's Church** and turn right down the road past the church to a gate and stile leading to a grassy track. Skirt the foot of the fell along this track. Below **Rake How** pass a ruined farm surrounded by sycamores and a giant overhanging yew.

4 Keep along this track, taking a high route right of and above **Sosgill**, to pass through three gates/stiles followed by a kissing gate into a **plantation**. Continue along a narrower, rocky path and skirt just above **Low Bridge End Farm** (a tea room and garden are at the far end). Continue along the path through another series of gates and stiles until it briefly touches the bank of **St John's Beck**, beneath **Wren Crag**. The path soon climbs again, traversing a steep slope falling straight down to the river (take care here). Swing right across a bracken-covered shoulder and down to the stile that leads back to the **A591**. Turn left and left again to return to the **car park** at Legburthwaite.

what to look for

Guarding the entrance to St John's in the Vale, the great volcanic plug of Castle Rock forms a daunting and impressive landmark. Jim Birkett (the writer of this walk's father) was the first to climb its sheer north face, some 200ft (61m) high, on 1 April 1939, by a route known as Overhanging Bastion and the crag has since become very popular for rock-climbing.

The surrounding hills reflected in the still waters of Thirlmere reservoir

The King's Head Hotel & Inn

WALK

Stunning Lakeland scenery surrounds this 17th-century former coaching inn which stands at the foot of Helvellyn. Inside, old oak beams and inglenook fireplaces with winter log fires are traditional features of the rambling main bar and intimate dining area, while on warm days the garden is the best place to enjoy a meal or a drink, with views of Blencathra and Skiddaw. Real ales and fine wine are served with the excellent food (bar food available throughout the day), offering good value for money. Comfortable en suite bedrooms for those wishing to linger to explore this beautiful area.

Food

In addition to sandwiches and cold platters, bar food may include chilli crab cakes, steamed pork belly, braised minted joint of lamb, and salmon grilled with thyme, basil and lemon grass. Round off with apple and pear crumble or a plate of local cheeses. Separate restaurant menu.

Family facilities

Children are welcome in the bars and overnight. There's a children's menu, big-screen TV in the bar, and a toy box. Super summer garden.

Alternative refreshment stops

There's a tea room and garden at Low Bridge End Farm, near the end of the walk. For those with very young children this makes a good objective for a shorter walk: simply reverse the directions of the last stage of the described walk.

about the pub

The King's Head Hotel & Inn
Thirlspot, Keswick
Cumbria CA12 4TN
Tel 01768772393
www.lakedistrictinns.co.uk

DIRECTIONS: 1 mile (1.6km) south of Legburthwaite, on the A591

PARKING: 50

OPEN: daily, all day

FOOD: daily, all day

BREWERY/COMPANY: free house

REAL ALE: Jennings Bitter, Theakston Bitter and Old Peculier

DOGS: not allowed inside

ROOMS: 17 en suite

☛ Where to go from here

Threlkeld Quarry and Mining Museum, near Keswick, tells the story of mining in the Cumbria of old when coal, gypsum, graphite, lead, copper, zinc and many other minerals were extracted from the land.

Legburthwaite · CUMBRIA

Bouth and Oxen Park

An action-packed short ride, with an exciting off-road option.

A wooded landscape

Magnificent woodland, dominated by sessile oak, is a major feature of this ride. Cyclists on the longer route who take the climb to Ickenthwaite will have plenty of time to appreciate this. In earlier times these woods were an industrial resource, providing raw materials for the bobbin industry and for charcoal-making to feed the many small iron makers in the area. Near the start of the ride, Moss Wood and the adjoining Height Springs Wood are now maintained by the

Woodland Trust. The track into Moss Wood is a bridleway so you could easily ride in a short way to get a closer look. You will see areas where the trees have been coppiced. This seemingly drastic operation involves cutting the tree back almost to ground level, but does not kill the plant. Instead it puts out many small shoots which in a few years provide thin timber ideal for both bobbin-making and charcoal-burning.

Just beyond the Manor House Inn in Oxen Park, you pass a grey barn-like building beside the road. Note the carved sign on the wall, which dates it to 1697, and portrays a selection of blacksmith's implements. Incidentally, a blacksmith is a general ironworker, who would largely have been involved in producing tools – one whose main job is shoeing horses is strictly called a farrier.

the ride

1 Follow the lane north, away from Bouth. Keep left at the first junction, signed to Oxen Park. The lane twists up through **woodland**, with a couple of quite sharp sections of climbing, passing the entrance to **Moss Wood**, before levelling out. At the next junction there is a triangle of grass.

Top: The Vale of Colton, crossed by a narrow road

Below left: Cyclist on a track between dry-stone walls

2 For the shorter ride go left here, signed to Oxen Park. The road twists and descends, crosses a little valley, then begins a steep twisting climb. As climbs go, this is not too long. Over the top, freewheel a short way to a T-junction on the outskirts of Oxen Park. Turn left to rejoin the longer loop shortly after Point 5.

For the longer route, keep right at Point 2, signposted 'Rusland: Gated Road'. Follow this lane until it drops to a T-junction. There's no need, but those with mountain-biking blood in their veins may not be able to resist splashing through the ford under the trees just before the junction. Turn right on the wider road, signed to **Grizedale**, and follow it for 0.75 mile (1.2km). Shortly after passing the elegant **Whitestock Hall**, look for a sharp left turn, signed to Ickenthwaite.

3 This leads immediately into a very steep climb, so engage low gear in advance. The gradient eventually eases and then the woods give way to fields.

| 2h00 | 7.75 MILES | 12.5 KM | LEVEL 123 |

SHORTER ALTERNATIVE ROUTE

| 1h00 | 4.5 MILES | 7.2 KM | LEVEL 12 |

MAP: OS Explorer OL 7 The English Lakes (SE)

START/FINISH: lane north of Bouth; grid ref: SD 328859

TRAILS/TRACKS: quiet lanes; rough tracks on longer ride, short challenging descents

LANDSCAPE: mix of woods and pasture, many small hills, views to higher fells

PUBLIC TOILETS: none on route

TOURIST INFORMATION: Ulverston, tel 01229 587120

CYCLE HIRE: South Lakeland Mountain Bike Sales & Hire, Lowick Bridge, Ulverston, tel 01229 885210; Wheelbase, Staveley, tel 01539 821443

THE PUB: White Hart Inn, Bouth, see Point **1** on route

🚫 Steep gradients on both loops. Shorter loop, suitability: children 7+. On longer loop, off-road descents require experience and skill, or walk short sections, suitability: children 12+. Mountain bike recommended

Getting to the start

Bouth is 1.25 miles (2km) north of the A590. Park in a grassy lay-by on the northern edge of the village, beyond the pub, or further along the lane on the first part of the ride.

Why do this cycle ride?

This short ride packs in a lot, in an area that's pure Lake District yet never inundated with visitors. For every climb there's a pleasant descent, and a new view to enjoy.

Researched and written by: Jon Sparks

4 Just after **Low Ickenthwaite** turn left on to a bridleway signed to Oxen Park. The track is initially stony with a good ribbon of grass down the middle. After a second gate it becomes stonier but is still straightforward. Stay close to the wall on the left, ignoring a couple of branch tracks. The track then climbs a bit on to an open, bracken-covered area. The best riding is generally in the centre of the track as the sides are quite rough. Go through another gate, and a little more climbing leads to the crest. Keep straight ahead at another fork and the track levels off. A short steep section at the start of the descent calls for some skill. If in doubt, walk down this. Then descend more steeply to another gate. The twisting descent beyond this is steep and loose and requires great care. Again, walk down rather than risk a nasty fall. Just beyond its foot is another gate.

5 Emerge on to a road and turn right into **Oxen Park**. As you enter the village, the shorter ride joins in from the left. Keep straight ahead through the village. The road begins a sweeping descent into the soft green **Vale of Colton**.

6 Just after the **Old Vicarage** turn left, signposted 'Colton Church and Bouth', up a short steep climb. At the crest another sign to Colton Church and Bouth points left, up a further climb. But this is an off-road route, so continue straight on. Descend to pass **Greenhead Farm**, and the road is fairly level along the valley side. Keep left through two junctions. The road curves and makes a steep final drop to a T-junction (take care). Go left for an almost level run along a broader road back through **Bouth**.

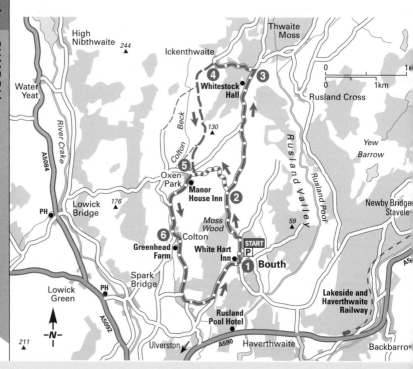

White Hart Inn

about the pub

White Hart Inn
Bouth, Ulverston
Cumbria LA12 8JB
Tel 01229 861229
www.edirectory.co.uk/whitehartinn

DIRECTIONS: in the middle of the village	
PARKING: 30	
OPEN: closed Monday and Tuesday lunchtime; open all day Saturday and Sunday, July–September	
FOOD: daily	
BREWERY/COMPANY: free house	
REAL ALE: Jennings Cumberland Ale, Black Sheep Bitter, Tetley, 3 guest beers	
ROOMS: 4 en suite	

A 16th-century former coaching inn, the White Hart is in a quiet village among woods, fields and fells. Sloping beamed ceilings and floors in the main bar show the building's age, while two log fires help create a cosy and welcoming atmosphere. Walls and ceilings are festooned with bric-a-brac and old photos – look out for the farm tools, stuffed animals and long-stemmed clay pipes. The landlord has a genuine passion for real ale, with six great ales, including brews from Cumbrian micro-breweries, to draw the customers in. He refuses to allow vinegar in the bar as it 'affects the quality of the beer'. A pub that has its priorities right! Upstairs there's a more open feel to the restaurant, with a large window giving it a fine outlook, shared with the rear terrace. The terrace has heaters for those chillier days, and a pleasant view of pastures and the wooded flanks of Colton Fell.

Food

The menu offers fresh food cooked to order using beef, pork and lamb from Abbots Reading Farm, a few miles away. Typically, this might include steak and stout pie, lamb and apricot pie, and pork medallions in port and mushroom sauce. Expect also soups, salads, sandwiches and pizzas.

Family facilities

Children are welcome in the eating areas and games room, and there's a limited children's menu. Play area on the village green opposite.

Alternative refreshment stops

The Manor House pub in Oxen Park (Point 5).

☛ Where to go from here

Lakeside is the steamer stop at the southern end of Lake Windermere and the starting point for the Lakeside and Haverthwaite Railway (www.windermere-lakecruises.co.uk). A short steam trip runs to Haverthwaite and there's a small collection of steam and diesel locomotives. Next door the fascinating Aquarium of the Lakes is well worth a visit (www.aquariumofthelakes.co.uk).

Bouth CUMBRIA

Grizedale Forest Park and Satterthwaite

A great circuit of the forest park.

Grizedale Forest

The speed and near-silence of a bike sometimes gives you some great wildlife encounters. We were privileged to see a family of foxes playing in the first few miles of this route. This may be exceptional, but deer – both red and roe – are widespread in the forest, and the sight of a buzzard overhead is almost guaranteed. (Buzzards are occasionally mistaken for eagles, but if you see a large bird of prey circling over this forest, it's a buzzard.) In spring the

courtship flights of these big birds of prey are beautiful to watch, and you may also see them being mobbed or harassed by other birds.

In the second half of the route there are great views west to the Coniston Fells. The principal peak at the southern end of the range is the Coniston Old Man (originally Allt Maen, meaning a high stone or cairn). To its left you glimpse the rock buttresses of Dow Crag, one of the great rock-climbers' crags of England. The sides of the Coniston Fells are heavily scarred, most obviously by slate quarries, but also by the copper mines which worked for around 500 years, reaching their peak in the 19th century.

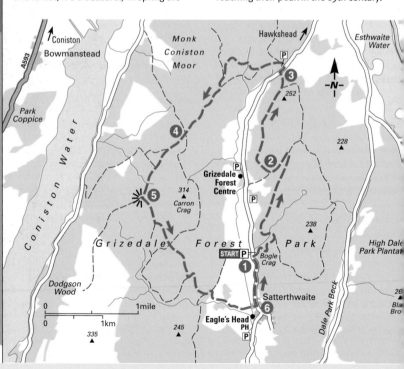

Cycling along a trail in Grizedale Forest

the ride

1 At the top of **Bogle Crag car park** go round the barrier and straight up the rocky track at a steady gradient. At a junction of tracks bear left, and enjoy a brief downhill respite and a fairly level section before some more steady climbing, sustained but never really steep. Where this eases off, turn left (**purple route marker**).

2 At the next fork keep right on the easy forest road, which sweeps round to the right (the left branch is a bridleway which makes a steep, rocky, experts-only descent direct to the Grizedale Forest visitor centre). After some undulations there's a longer downhill, then another substantial climb, quite steep to start. Just over the top, reach a junction of tracks. Go left and gently downhill to a **gate**. The most challenging part of the uphill section is now over.

3 Go round the gate on the left, with care as the ground is rocky. Come out to the road and turn right. After 200yds (183m) turn left at **Moor Top**. Go through the **car park** and immediately beyond the barrier

— **2h00** — **9.5 MILES** — **15.3 KM** — **LEVEL 1 2 3** —

MAP: OS Explorer OL 7 The English Lakes (SE)

START/FINISH: Bogle Crag car park, Grizedale Forest; grid ref: SD 337933

TRAILS/TRACKS: forest tracks with mostly good surface, short sections of field track and lane

LANDSCAPE: forest, with views to the fells

PUBLIC TOILETS: Grizedale Forest Centre

TOURIST INFORMATION: Hawkshead, tel 015394 36525

CYCLE HIRE: Grizedale Mountain Bikes, Grizedale, tel 01229 860369

THE PUB: The Eagles Head, Satterthwaite, see Point **6** on route

🛈 Some moderately steep descents with loose surfaces. Suitability: children 12+. Mountain bike recommended. (Other waymarked routes in the forest are shorter and easier)

Getting to the start

Grizedale Forest lies to the east of Coniston Water, with the village of Grizedale at its heart. Bogle Crag car park is 0.75 mile (1.2km) south of the village on the only road through the valley, and 0.5 mile (800m) north of Satterthwaite.

Why do this cycle ride?

Grizedale Forest Park has many waymarked cycle routes on the forest roads, as well as a pre-existing network of bridleways, some of which offer much tougher riding (strictly for hardened mountain-bikers). The route makes for a fine day out, and gives a fair sample of what the forest has to offer.

Researched and written by: Jon Sparks

fork left. Pass a small lake (**Juniper Tarn**) in the trees on the left and at the next fork go right. Curve round the head of a small valley and climb fairly gently, keeping straight on where another track joins from the right. At the next junction keep right. The next section is broadly level, past stands of **younger trees**. Pass an area of broadleaf planting (mostly birch) and get the first view of the **Coniston Fells** away to the right. Continue, to reach a double junction, almost a crossroads.

4 Bear left and then right to maintain the same general direction. Keep on along the **main track**, past several turnings descending to the right, until an obvious track forks off down to the right. There's a **bench** here, with a great view of the full length of the **Coniston Fells**. It's a perfect place to pause for a drink or snack, or just to enjoy the panorama.

5 Ignore the descending track and keep on along the level one. Soon there's a small rise and the track swings round to the left. A bridleway breaks off to the right here – another classic mountain bike route. Keep straight on and descend, passing another track that branches off to the right. At the next junction keep left (**green waymark**). This section is quite loose, so take care. Keep straight on at the next junction – a narrower track on the right makes it a crossroads. There's more fast descent through **mature forest** – the surface here is mostly good, but gets looser as you drop to a T-junction. Turn left and continue the descent, winding down through **broadleaf woods**. Keep left at the next junction, over a slight rise, then look out for a right turn (easy to miss) just before the track reaches fields on the right. Follow this slightly rougher track down to a gate and then through fields. It's bumpy in places as it descends to another gate,

Sculpture of a man with an axe in the undergrowth at Grizedale Forest

then continue across the level valley floor. The village of **Satterthwaite** is ahead. There's a short rise, with bedrock visible, before you meet the road.

6 Turn left here for a direct return to **Bogle Crag car park**, or turn right for 400yds (366m) to **The Eagles Head** pub.

The Eagles Head

about the pub

The Eagles Head
Satterthwaite, Ulverston
Cumbria LA12 8LN
Tel 01229 860237

DIRECTIONS: in the centre of the village, just south of the church
PARKING: 8
OPEN: closed Monday lunchtime
FOOD: no food Monday evening
BREWERY/COMPANY: free house
REAL ALE: Barngates Cracker Ale, Hawkshead Gold, guest beer

'Walkers and cyclists are always welcome, however muddy.' That comment sums up the unpretentious Eagles Head. And on some of the rougher routes in Grizedale, it is understood that mountain-bikers can get very muddy indeed. This fine pub says it is 'In the Heart of the Grizedale Forest', and that seems to be true in more senses than the purely geographical. The interior is warm and cosy in a style typical of many a Lakeland hostelry, complete with slate floor, log fires and simple furnishings. On a fine day there is intense competition for tables in the small but delightful garden, with its sheltering trees and flower-decked walls. Additional attractions include tip-top local ales, in particular Barngates Cracker Ale.

Food

There are separate lunchtime and evening menus, with good quality sandwiches (home-roast ham and cheese), filled jacket potatoes and leek and mushroom crumble at lunchtime. Some main course dishes, like home-made steak, chicken or game pies, overlap on both menus, but the evening selection ranges more widely, with a good choice of curry dishes among others.

Family facilities

Families are made very welcome.

Alternative refreshment stops

Café at the Grizedale Forest visitor centre; pubs and cafés in nearby Hawkshead.

☛ Where to go from here

Admire an annually changing exhibition of Beatrix Potter's paintings used to illustrate her children's books, often incorporating local scenes, at the Beatrix Potter Gallery, Hawkshead (tel 015394 36355).

Grizedale CUMBRIA

Up Souther Fell from Mungrisdale

WALK

Rolling grassy fells offer quiet solitude and an air of intrigue.

Souther Fell

With a theatrical air the River Glenderamackin weaves a circuitous course around Souther (pronounced Sowter) Fell, passing through the hamlet of Mungrisdale (pronounced Mun-grize-dul). Whereas the central Lakeland fells are composed of hard volcanic rocks, Souther Fell and its neighbouring hills are made up of the relatively soft rocks of Skiddaw slate. The resultant smooth and rounded terrain of this mountain region gives an air of wild desolation.

Locals have long said that a ghostly spectral army of warriors marches over Souther Fell on Midsummer's Eve. Sightings peaked in 1745, the year the Jacobite Scot, Prince Charles Edward Stuart (Bonnie Prince Charlie), marched on England.

On the evening before midsummer, and following reports that soldiers and horsemen had been seen marching along the high shoulder of Souther Fell, a group of 26 men stationed themselves at a suitable vantage point in the valley, determined to lay low the rumours and speculation. To their disbelief, the sceptics witnessed a rapidly moving line of troops, horses and carriages, spreading right across the high shoulder of the fell in a continuous chain. Steep places and rocky outcrops neither slowed nor disrupted the progress of this huge army. The men couldn't believe their eyes, yet only darkness put an effective end to these strange events.

The next day there was no further sign of the great army. With considerable trepidation, and half expecting that the threatened invasion of Scots had begun, a party climbed to the summit – where they found nothing. Not a mark in the grass, no footprint, hoof-print or wheel rut, and no sign of an army sheltering in the valley below. Yet the 26 were convinced they had seen an army, and determined that their integrity should be respected, swearing an oath before a magistrate as to what they had seen.

The Scots did invade – but not until November of that year. The truth remains a mystery.

Below: Looking across the hills and valleys towards Eden Valley and the North Pennines
Right: Cairn on Souther Fell looking towards Blencathra

what to look for

The charming little church that takes its name from St Mungo ('the loved one') is next to the road in the village, and worth inspection. St Mungo, who also went by the name of St Kentigern, and became the Bishop of Glasgow, is thought to have been a missionary from Ireland who preached at a number of churches in Cumbria during the 10th century.

For solitude and contemplation there are few more rewarding places to visit than the tiny Church of St Kentigern (or St Mungo) at nearby Castle Sowerby. It's not easy to find, but the views of the fells from here are sublime.

he walk

Head north up the road, with a glimpse of The Mill Inn across the river. Where e road takes a sharp bend back to the ght, turn left by the **phone box**, and follow e little lane between the **cottages**. Go rough the gate and continue along the nsurfaced track above the north bank of e **River Glenderamackin**. Bear left and ross **Bullfell Beck** by a narrow footbridge.

As the main track starts to climb steeply, bear left on a lesser stony path which aces a route along the right bank (true left) f the **River Glenderamackin**. The going is raightforward although the path has been roded in places and there is a steep drop to the little river. Continue along the track, ith some boggy stretches, to cross annerdale Beck on easy stepping stones. nore a zigzag path climbing on the right – is goes to **Bannerdale Crags**. The path is asier now, broad and grassy, further from e river. The gradient eases as it rounds e shoulder of Bannerdale Crags (named hite Horse Bent by the Ordnance Survey). oon a path bears down left to a flat ooden footbridge across the **River lenderamackin,** which is barely 6ft (2m) ide at this point.

3h00	6 MILES	9.7 KM	LEVEL 1 2 3

MAP: OS Explorer OL 5 The English Lakes (NE)

START/FINISH: wide verge above river, Mungrisdale village; grid ref: NY 364300

PATHS: grassy and stony paths, open fellside, 4 stiles

LANDSCAPE: remote river valley, open exposed fellside

PUBLIC TOILETS: none on route

TOURIST INFORMATION: Keswick, tel 017687 72645

THE PUB: The Mill Inn, Mungrisdale, near start of route

⚠ Steep rocky descent near the end of the walk. Suitability: children 8+

Getting to the start

Mungrisdale is signposted off the A66 between Penrith and Keswick, 9 miles (14.5km) west of Penrith. The best parking is on wide grass verges about 200yds (183m) past the Mungrisdale village sign.

Researched and written by:
Bill Birkett, Jon Sparks

WALK

Souther Fell

CUMBRIA

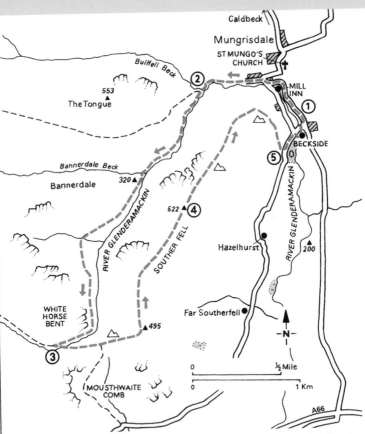

3 The path ascends diagonally left to a high grassy saddle. Turn left to ascend the long shoulder of **Souther Fell**, keeping left at successive forks. When the path forks again in a slight dip, keep left to reach a large **cairn** of Skiddaw slate with splashes of white quartz. Continue along the near-level ridge to a rounded rise with rock peeping through – the summit.

4 Keep north and continue to descend the grassy nose of the fell. Easy at first, the angle steepens progressively until, nearing the base, the path twists down through outcrops with some rock steps. Watch out for a **post** with a white waymark indicating an ill-defined path slanting down right to a **clump of trees**.

(If you miss this, simply follow the transverse wall at the bottom, along to the trees.) From the trees, continue along the wall, grassed-over in places and topped by a fence, until it bends left and a short descent leads to a tarmac lane.

5 Go left, through a gate and down the road. At the bottom of the hill, a grassy track continues on down to the **river**. If the water's very low, you could ford the river here. Normally, just before the ford, climb concrete steps over the wall on the right to reach a narrow footbridge. Cross the bridge and then go left and over a squeeze stile. Go up to the road and turn left to return to the **parking area**.

The Mill Inn

about the pub

The Mill Inn
Mungrisdale, Penrith
Cumbria CA11 0XR
Tel 01687 79632
www.the-millinn.co.uk

DIRECTIONS: south of St Mungo's Church, Mungrisdale
PARKING: 40
OPEN: daily, all day
FOOD: daily
BREWERY/COMPANY: free house
REAL ALE: Jennings Bitter and Cumberland Ale, guest beer
DOGS: welcome in the bar
ROOMS: 6 en suite

The 16th-century Mill Inn sits right at the foot of Souther Fell in a secluded village, towards the end of the walk you get a bird's eye view of your final destination. Private ground forces a long detour to the right, but it's worth the effort. The pub is a long, low building of whitewashed stone with a slate roof. Inside, you will find low-beamed ceilings, an open fire in a stone fireplace, and an old millstone by the wooden bar. Not only is the pub the hub of the community, it is a great walkers' pub and draws visitors from far afield for home-cooked dishes using fresh local ingredients. You'll get a peaceful sleep in one of six rooms.

Food

All the hoped-for favourites are here (lunchtime sandwiches and ploughman's lunches, home-made pies, scampi and chips), while the specials menu offers more elaborate dishes such as grilled fresh salmon with a mushroom, white wine and cream sauce or pan-fried duck breast with honey, port and coriander.

Family facilities

Children are very welcome in the games room and eating areas and there is a lovely garden beside a rumbling brook to relax in during the summer months.

☛ Where to go from here

Take the A66 east and visit Rheged –The Village in the Hill. This incredible attraction is Europe's largest grass-covered building, designed to look like a Lakeland hill. Inside is a cinema and a exhibition on mountaineering (www.rheged.com).

Loughrigg Fell from Ambleside

Above the town, Loughrigg Fell looks out to lake, dale and high fell.

Ambleside

Even before the spectacularly beautiful heights of Loughrigg are reached, the varied slate stone buildings of Ambleside provide an intriguing start to this walk. There is a lot more to this little town than just being the outdoor equipment capital of Britain. Ambleside has long been a site of occupation. Bronze Age remains, c2000 BC can be seen on the nearby fells and the Galava Roman fort, near Waterhead, was one of the most important in north west England.

How Head, just up the Kirkstone road, one of the oldest surviving buildings in Ambleside, is located in the area known as Above Stock. Sections of this fine stone house date back to the 16th century, and it was once the lodge of the Master Forester of the Barony of Kendal. It has massive circular chimneys, a typical Westmorland feature, and stone mullioned windows. It even incorporates stone from the old Roman fort at Waterhead and cobbles from the bed of Stock Ghyll Beck.

Stock Ghyll was the heartbeat of the town when, some 150 years ago, it provided water power for 12 mills. On this walk you'll pass a restored waterwheel, immediately followed by the famous Bridge House, one of the most photographed buildings in the Lake District. Spanning the beck, this tiny 17th-century building is said to have been built thus to avoid paying land tax. Locally it is said to have once housed a family with six children. It is now a shop and information centre for the National Trust.

the walk

1 Take the wooden footbridge from the car park and go right, to pass the waterwheel and **Bridge House**. At the junction turn right down **Compston Road**. Halfway down, by **Zeffirelli's**, bear right and down **Vicarage Road** towards the church. Pass the school and enter **Rothay Park**. Follow the main path through the park to emerge by a flat bridge over **Stock Ghyll Beck**. Cross this, then go left to cross over the stone arched **Miller Bridge** spanning the **River Rothay**.

2 Turn right along the road over the cattle grid and then turn left on a steep tarmac lane. Climb the lane to the building of **Brow Head**. At the next sharp bend, climb steps to a path running horizontally left to a squeeze-stile, a footbridge and

The stone Bridge House, now a National Trust information centre, spans Stock Ghyll

a gate. A few steps start the main path up the open hillside above. This soon forks: bear left, rising across the slope before climbing more directly up a tiny valley and then up a rocky knoll to a **cairn** and the first view of **Windermere**. Follow the ridge over two more knolls, with views of the **Coniston Fells** ahead and the **Fairfield Horseshoe** to the right.

3 Drop down right to a cairn in a pool (sometimes dry), then follow a well-defined path which soon bears left, over a rise and down to lovely little pocket-handkerchief **Lily Tarn** (flowers bloom late June to September). The path curves gently left, round the tarn, then fairly straight, meeting a wall on the left. Descend close to the wall, past a kissing gate, into a dip. Follow a choice of paths up the rocky slope ahead to another worthy viewpoint.

4 Drop down to a small **pool** (more lilies) then turn right on a grassy path. Descend towards a stand of **conifers** and

The view across Ambleside from Loughrigg Fell

1h45	**3.25 MILES**	**5.3 KM**	**LEVEL 2**

PATHS: OS Explorer OL 7 The English Lakes (SE)

START/FINISH: central pay-and-display car park, Ambleside; grid ref: NY 375047

PATHS: road, paths and tracks, can be muddy in places, 3 stiles

LANDSCAPE: town, park and open hillside with views to high fells

PUBLIC TOILETS: at car park

TOURIST INFORMATION: Ambleside, tel: 01539 432582

THE PUB: Queen's Hotel, Ambleside

🛈 There are innumerable tracks on Loughrigg Fell, and navigation can be tricky in poor visibility. Suitability: children 6+

Getting to the start

In Ambleside follow signs for Keswick round the one-way system. The main car park is located on the left, shortly after passing the distinctive landmark of Bridge House.

Researched and written by:
Bill Birkett, Jon Sparks

WALK

bear right to a gate close by the trees. Go through the gate and descend the stony track. This area was once a golf course and the first house was the clubhouse. Intercept the original route just above the buildings of **Brow Head**.

5 Continue to cross **Miller Bridge** then, before the flat bridge, bear left to follow the track by the side of **Stock Ghyll Beck**. Beyond the meadows a lane through the houses leads to the main **Rydal road**. Bear right along the road to the car park beyond the fire station.

what to look for

Lily Tarn, just after Point 3, is naturally known for its water lilies. The lilies have lightly scented white flowers that unfurl between June and September. Despite its great beauty the flower has a sinister reputation. While its blooms may tempt the inquisitive, its rope-like stems, which grow up to 8ft (2.4m) long, can easily ensnare the unwary, and many a hapless swimmer has been drowned, beguiled by its innocent appearance.

Ambleside CUMBRIA

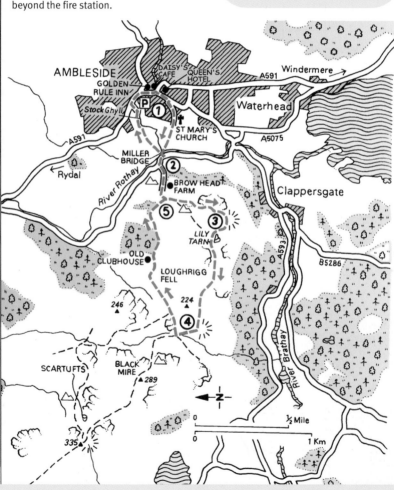

Queen's Hotel

about the pub

Queen's Hotel
Market Place, Ambleside
Cumbria LA22 9BU
Tel 015394 32206
www.queenshotelambleside.com

22

WALK

A short walk from the main car park and right in the heart of the busy Market Place stands the Queen's Hotel. It is spacious and clean, and a friendly welcome ensures it doesn't have the antiseptic feel that some larger hotels convey. It is also a popular 'free house', with a lively bar, replete with roaring log fire and good quality real ale from Cumbria breweries on tap, and a comfortable lounge area where freshly cooked meals are served. At weekends the cellar bar is open (Sky TV).

DIRECTIONS:	Market Place is in the centre of Ambleside
PARKING:	use walk car park
OPEN:	daily, all day
FOOD:	daily, all day
BREWERY/COMPANY:	free house
REAL ALE:	Yates, Jennings, Moorhouses, Hawkshead, guest beer
DOGS:	welcome in the bars only
ROOMS:	26 en suite

Ambleside CUMBRIA

Food

The lunch menu is served all afternoon and offers sandwiches, hot ciabatta bread filled with Cumberland sausage, home-made soup, jacket potatoes with various fillings, and traditional burgers. From the main menu you can order steak and ale pie, freshly battered cod, the daily roast, or rump steak with all the trimmings.

Family facilities

Children are welcome throughout the hotel and a menu is available for those with smaller appetites. Patio to the rear for summer eating and drinking.

Alternative refreshment stops

Inns, cafés and restaurants and all types of eateries abound in Ambleside. Favourites with walkers and climbers include Daisy's Café, opposite the market cross.

☞ Where to go from here

The Armitt Museum, opposite the car park, provides a fascinating look at Ambleside and its environs in times past. Borrans Park at Waterhead, with Galava Roman fort next to it, and Rothay Park provide pleasant recreational areas for those with a little time to spare. Near Bridge House, Adrian Sankey Glass Makers provides demonstrations in glass-blowing.

A circuit around Cartmel

Explore a handsome valley between the fells and the sea.

Cartmel

There have been buildings on the site of Cartmel Priory for more than 800 years, though only the church and the gatehouse remain standing today. One of the most striking features of the notably beautiful church is the number of memorials to travellers who lost their lives crossing Morecambe Bay. In the days before railways and modern roads, the sands of the bay were in regular use by travellers of all kinds, and an official Queen's Guide was charged with ensuring their safety.

Those who dispensed with his services risked blundering into quicksand or being caught by the fast-advancing tides – hazards which are still very real. The office of Queen's Guide survives to this day, and visitors are still guided safely across these treacherous sands every year.

Horse racing at Cartmel also has a long tradition behind it, and the meetings around the late May and August bank holidays draw horses, jockeys and punters from far and wide for an exciting day out. However, busy roads on race days mean these times are best avoided by cyclists.

The church at Cartmel Priory with its square tower set diagonally

the ride

1 From the **racecourse** ride back into **Cartmel village square** and turn sharp left (round the village shop). This quickly takes you out of the village again and alongside the racecourse. Keep left at a junction, following signs for Haverthwaite and Ulverston, and begin a steady climb (never really steep). The road forks again at **Beck Side**.

2 Keep on to the right, still climbing steadily. The limestone arch on the right just above the fork is the remains of a **lime kiln**. There's a brief dip at **High Gateside**, another short rise, then turn right and begin an excellent swooping descent, with no tricky bends.

3 A turn on the right at a triangle of grass offers the option of a short return back to Cartmel. Otherwise, keep straight on here, and at a second junction. Cross the tiny river of **Ayside Pool** (pool as the word for a river occurs several places hereabouts), then up slightly to reach a T-junction. Turn left on a broader road and continue for about 0.5 mile (800m), passing **Field Broughton church**, whose spire dominates the upper part of the valley just as Cartmel Priory does the lower.

4 At the next junction fork right, signed to **Barber Green**, and keep left where the road splits again. At a tiny crossroads under a spreading beech tree turn right, following signs for Barber Green. Ascend gently through the village of **Barber Green**, then

1h00 · **8 MILES** · **12.9 KM** · **LEVEL 1 2 3**

MAP: OS Explorer OL 7 The English Lakes (SE)

START/FINISH: Cartmel racecourse; grid ref: SD 375791

TRAILS/TRACKS: country lanes, some wider roads. Avoid doing this ride when race meetings are on

LANDSCAPE: wide valley flanked by ridges, with views to the higher fells and to Morecambe Bay

PUBLIC TOILETS: Cartmel

TOURIST INFORMATION: Ulverston, tel: 01229 587120

CYCLE HIRE: South Lakeland Mountain Bike Sales and Hire, Lowick Bridge, Ulverston, tel: 01229 885210

THE PUB: Cavendish Arms, Cartmel, see Point **6** on route

🛑 Railway path section is suitable for all ages. If continuing into Threlkeld, suitability: children 6+; if returning via stone circle there's a short section (walk on pavement) alongside busy A road, and crossing another. Suitability: children 10+

Getting to the start
Cartmel is 2 miles (3.2km) west of Grange-over-Sands. The racecourse is west of the village square, and there's an honesty-box at the car park there.

Why do this cycle ride?
The Vale of Cartmel is a classic English landscape, its skylines punctuated by nothing more obtrusive than a church tower. Add views of the high Lakeland fells and the shining expanse of Morecambe Bay, and there are few better rides for scenic variety.

Researched and written by: Jon Sparks

the road climbs more seriously again. Keep straight on at the crossroads just beyond the village. The next bit is steeper, but as you near the top there's a great view to the right down the valley, with the **tower** of the priory standing out and the sweep of Morecambe Bay beyond. Finally, the climb levels off. Just beyond this, reach a T-junction on the outskirts of **High Newton**.

5 Turn right and shortly keep right at a fork by the aptly named **Valley View**. Descend (another fine run) past **Head House**. Keep straight on at the crossroads of **Four Lane Ends**. After 0.5 mile (800m) reach an angled junction with a wider road. Keep left (almost straight ahead) for an easy run back to **Cartmel**.

6 About 200yds (183m) past the 30mph sign on the edge of Cartmel, turn right at an 'Unsuitable for heavy goods vehicles' sign. Follow the narrowing lane between

cottages and past the back of the **Priory**, then loop round and past the **Cavendish Arms**. Go under the gatehouse arch into the village square. Take the lane left of the village shop back to the **racecourse**.

Bust of Sir William Lowther, Cartmel Priory

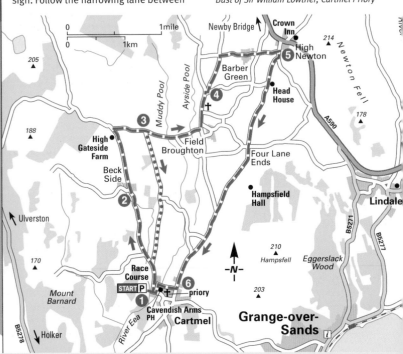

Cavendish Arms

Cartmel's oldest hostelry dates from the 15th century and stands tucked away from the village square. It is built within the old village walls and was once a thriving coaching stop, with stables where the bar is now. Note the mounting block dated 1837 outside the main door. The civilised main bar has low oak beams, a comfortable mixture of furnishings, Jennings ale on tap, a good selection of wines by glass or bottle, and welcoming log fires burn on cooler days. There is a separate non-smoking restaurant, and ten well appointed bedrooms.

about the pub

Cavendish Arms
Cavendish Street, Cartmel
Grange-over-Sands,
Cumbria LA11 6QA
Tel 015395 36240
www.thecavendisharms.co.uk

DIRECTIONS: off the main square	
PARKING: 15	
OPEN: daily, all day	
FOOD: daily, all day Saturday and Sunday; no food Sunday evening in winter	
BREWERY/COMPANY: free house	
REAL ALE: Jennings Bitter, Wells Bombardier, guest beer	
ROOMS: 10 en suite	

Food
Bar food ranges from soup and sandwiches to lamb Henry, Cumberland sausages in a rich onion gravy and smoked haddock on black pudding mash. The dessert menu includes Cartmel's speciality, sticky toffee pudding. Typical restaurant dishes might be fillet steak, sea bass and ostrich.

Family facilities
Children are genuinely welcome. Children's menu is available, and the rear garden has small play area and a viewpoint from which to feed the ducks.

Alternative refreshment stops
Try the King's Arms, Royal Oak, Market Cross Cottage Tea Rooms or the Pig and Whistle Bistro in Cartmel. Close to the midpoint is the Crown Inn at High Newton.

☛ Where to go from here
There's plenty to see at Holker Hall, west of Cartmel at Cark, including magnificent gardens and the Lakeland Motor Museum (tel: 015395 58328; www.holker-hall.co.uk).

From Patterdale by Ullswater

Along the shores of
Ullswater silver point,
a spectacular viewpoint.

Ullswater

Ullswater is undoubtedly one of the
loveliest of the lakes. Its three arms add up
to a total length of 7.5 miles (12.1km) with
an average width of 0.5 mile (800m) and a
maximum depth of 205ft (62.5m). It is

Lakeland's second largest lake, not quite
measuring up to Windermere. Its waters are
exceptionally clear and in the deepest part
of the lake, off Howtown, lives a curious
fish called the schelly – a creature akin to
a freshwater herring.

Apart from rescue and Park Ranger
launches, you won't see many power boats
here, but Ullswater 'Steamers' have three
boats operating between Glenridding and
Pooley Bridge during the summer.

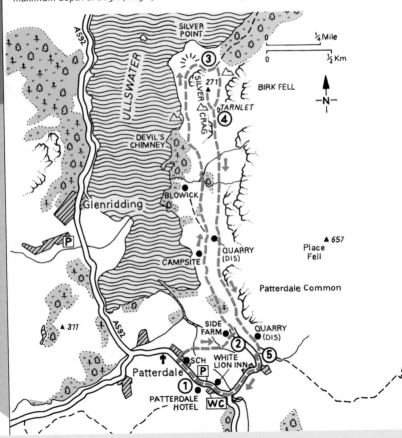

Alfred Wainwright (1907–91), known for his seven *Pictorial Guides to the Lakeland Fells*, regarded this to be a part of one of the most beautiful walks in the Lakes – a sentiment with which many would agree. Preservation of the lake in its present form is due to a concerted campaign, led in Parliament by Lord Birkett, against the proposed Manchester Corporation Water Act in 1965. Although the act was passed, and water is extracted from the lake, the workings are hidden underground and designed in such a way as to make it impossible to lower the water level beyond the agreed limit.

It was the sight of golden daffodils amongst the trees and beside the shore of this lake that inspired William Wordsworth's most widely known poem, 'I wandered lonely as a cloud' (1807). Wordsworth's sister Dorothy recorded the occasion vividly in her diary: 'I never saw daffodils so beautiful. They grew among the mossy stones about and around them, some rested their heads upon these stones as on a pillar for weariness and the rest tossed and reeled and danced and seemed as if they verily laughed with the wind that blew them over the lake.'

1h45 · **4 MILES** · **6.4 KM** · **LEVEL 2**

WALK

Patterdale CUMBRIA

PATHS: OS Explorer OL 5 The English Lakes (NE)

START/FINISH: pay-and-display car park, Patterdale; grid ref: NY 396159

PATHS: stony tracks and paths, no stiles

LANDSCAPE: lake and fell views, mixed woodland

PUBLIC TOILETS: opposite White Lion in Patterdale village centre

TOURIST INFORMATION: Ullswater (Glenridding), tel: 017684 82414

THE PUB: Patterdale Hotel, Patterdale, see Point **1** on route

🛈 Rough tracks with some steep sections. Suitability: children 8+

Getting to the start

Patterdale village lies at the southern tip of Ullswater, stretched along the A592. The car park is opposite the Patterdale Hotel.

Researched and written by:
Bill Birkett, Jon Sparks

Daffodils cluster along the shore of Ullswater

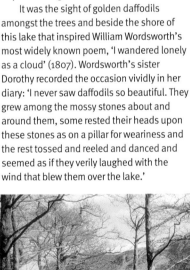

the walk

1 Walk out to the **main road**. Cross to gain the pavement and turn right. Opposite a sign for Side Farm cross back to a stony track, signed to Howtown and Boardale. Follow the track over a bridge and up between the buildings of **Side Farm**. Turn left on another roughly surfaced track.

2 Follow the undulating track, with a stone wall on your left. The lake head and **Glenridding** appear away to the left, with the lead mine remains prominent in the valley beyond. Continue on above the campsite and through further undulations before the path ascends again to crest a craggy knoll above the woods of **Devil's Chimney**. Make a steep rocky descent (care required) before the path levels to traverse beneath the craggy heights of Silver Crag. In places the steep ground falls directly to the lake below. A slight ascent, passing some fine holly trees, gains the shoulder of **Silver Point** and an outstanding view of **Ullswater**.

3 Follow the path, which sweeps round beneath the end of **Silver Crag**, until a steep stony path, eroded in places, breaks off to the right. Ascend this, climbing steeply through the juniper bushes, into the narrow gap which separates Silver Crag

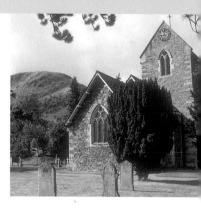

The small 19th-century Church of St Patrick in Patterdale with Helvellyn in the background

to the right from the main hillside of **Birk Fell** to the left. This little valley is quite boggy and holds a small tarn.

4 The path ahead soon begins a gradual descent back towards **Patterdale**. (If you have energy to spare, a short steep ascent leads to the top of Silver Crag – the view is not that much better than from Silver Point, but you are more likely to enjoy it in solitude. Where the main path levels out, climb steeply through a grassy gap between the crags. Bear right at the top on a narrow path through the prickly juniper, to the top. Descend by the same route to the main path.) The path traversing the open fell is easy, though it may be boggy in places. Pass above an old quarry, tree-filled and unfenced, and then descend across the slate spoil from another quarry. An artificial **cave** here usually has a waterfall spilling over its lip. Continue along the hillside above **Side Farm**, passing through more quarry workings. Descend to meet a wider track and follow it down to the right to a gate.

5 Go through the gate and bear left on a lane. Bear right at the next junction and through the meadows back to the main road. Turn right back into **Patterdale**.

what to look for

The distinctive golden yellow and white of the indigenous daffodil still abounds in the woods by the lakeshore and may be seen at its best from mid-March to mid-April. This wild variety is smaller than the cultivated version and, many would say, even more lovely. There has been concern recently that the introduction of cultivated daffodils to this area is actually damaging the survival prospects of its smaller relative and jeopardising the view Wordsworth loved.

Patterdale Hotel

WALK

about the pub

Patterdale Hotel
Patterdale, Ullswater
Cumbria CA11 0NN
Tel 017684 82231
www.patterdalehotel.co.uk

DIRECTIONS: in the centre of Patterdale village

PARKING: 40

OPEN: daily, all day

FOOD: daily, all day

BREWERY/COMPANY: Chace Hotels

REAL ALE: Jennings

DOGS: welcome in the garden only

This roadside hotel stands at the southern edge of Ullswater, with magnificent views of the valley and fells. Although it is a large hotel catering mainly for the tourist trade, its location also makes it a popular base for walkers, who are most welcome in the spacious and very comfortable main bar. Not only is it open all day, with food available throughout the day, but you'll find Jennings beer on tap and an extensive garden with super views across to Place Fell, along whose slopes this walk runs.

Food

Expect a wide range of traditional pub dishes, including local Cumberland sausage, pasta meals, ploughman's lunches and decent sandwiches. There's a separate restaurant menu – rack of lamb with herb crust and a redcurrant and port sauce or baked salmon supreme with lemon butter sauce, for example.

Family facilities

In keeping with most Lakeland hotels, families are made very welcome. Children are allowed in the bar, youngsters have their own menu to choose from, and the secluded and safe garden is great for kids to relax in.

Alternative refreshment stops

Side Farm sometimes offers teas and ice creams. In the centre of Patterdale, the White Lion Inn serves bar meals throughout the year, but its outdoor seating is very close to the road.

☛ Where to go from here

North along the A592 via a scenic 0.25 mile (400m) walk through National Trust woodland is Aira Force. This impressive waterfall is best seen just after rain or on a misty morning. Further along the A592, Dalemain House is set in stunning parkland. Its attractions include the Westmorland and Cumberland Yeomanry Museum, and a countryside collection in the 16th-century barn. The house has beautiful gardens and there's an adventure playground for children.

Patterdale CUMBRIA

Woods and water by Windermere

Along the peaceful western shore of England's largest lake.

Windermere

CUMBRIA

Windermere

A 10mph (16.1km) speed limit for powered craft on the lake comes into force in 2005, and should make this ride much more peaceful than previously. However, the limit has been controversial and may yet be defied. Other water traffic includes yachts of all sizes, windsurfers, canoes, rowing boats and the traditional launches and steamers which ply up and down throughout the year.

An attractive feature, the privately owned Belle Isle is said to have been used since Roman times. Today it is supplied by a little boat, which serves the 38 acre (15ha) estate. Belle Isle's circular house, recently rebuilt after extensive fire damage, was originally built by a Mr English in 1774. Apparently William Wordsworth accredited Mr English with the honour of being the first man to settle in the Lake District for the sake of the scenery.

The woodland here is typical of the Lake District. Before clearances for agriculture, notably sheep-grazing, there were many more similar woods. The predominant species is the sessile oak, which in times past provided timber for local industry and bark for tanning. It is a close relative of the 'English' oak of more southern counties, and it is not easy to tell them apart, but on closer inspection you will see that the acorns have no stalks to speak of. These woods are also rich in mosses and ferns, but often the most striking plant is the foxglove, which fills the clearings.

the ride

1 Leave the **car park** and turn left on a surfaced lane. There are views along here of moored yachts, **Belle Isle** and the lake, with a backdrop of high fells. The shapely peak is **Ill Bell**. Follow the lane past lay-bys to reach a gate and cattle grid.

2 The road beyond is marked 'Unsuitable for Motor Vehicles'. Keep left past the entrance to **Strawberry Gardens**. Beyond this the track becomes considerably rougher, and soon begins to climb quite steeply. It's worth persevering!

3 Once over the crest and just as you begin to descend, look out on the left

1h00 — **5.75 MILES** — **9.2 KM** — **LEVEL 2**

MAP:	OS Explorer OL 7 The English Lakes (SE)
START/FINISH:	car park near Windermere Ferry; grid ref: SD 387958
TRAILS/TRACKS:	mostly easy tracks, some stony sections
LANDSCAPE:	rich woodland and lakeshore
PUBLIC TOILETS:	none on route
TOURIST INFORMATION:	Bowness-on-Windermere, tel 015394 42895
CYCLE HIRE:	Wheelbase, Staveley, tel 01539 821443; Bike Treks, Ambleside, tel 01539 431245; Ghyllside Cycles, Ambleside, tel 01539 433592; Grizedale Mountain Bikes, Grizedale Forest, tel 01229 860369
THE PUB:	Sawrey Hotel, Far Sawrey, near start of route

🚴 Mostly easy but one rough steep climb and descent. Suitability: children 8+. Mountain bike recommended, or walk some sections. Shorter ride from Red Nab, all ages

Getting to the start

Road access to Windermere's mid-western shore is via Far Sawrey or on minor roads from the south. Follow the B5285 towards the ferry terminal, turning left up a lane before the terminal itself, to reach a National Trust car park. Alternatively, bring your bikes over by ferry from Bowness-on-Windermere.

Why do this cycle ride?

This is a perfect ride for taking a picnic. The full ride is surprisingly challenging, with a steep, rocky climb and descent halfway, though elsewhere the going is easy. For a shorter ride, go from the car park at Red Nab. Then follow the bridleway to High Wray Bay.

Researched and written by: Jon Sparks

for a **wildlife viewing platform**. There are squirrel feeders scattered in the trees, and you may spot roe deer. Take great care on the descent – there are loose stones and several rocky steps, and it may be safer to walk down. The track levels out for a short distance, then continues its descent, finally levelling out just above the lakeshore. The going is easier now, generally level. Pass several small **shingle beaches**. Keep left (almost straight ahead) at a fork and then, where a bridleway climbs off to the left, keep right (signed to **Red Nab** and **Wray**) along a smoother gravel track. At a gate, emerge onto a tarmac track but almost immediately fork right, signposted 'Bridleway Wray Castle'. Continue into the **Red Nab car park**.

Top: Windermere seen from Orrest Head

Tree-covered hills sloping down to Windermere from Gummers How

4 Go round a low barrier on to the bridleway. This is level, easy riding all the way along to a gate by a boathouse, beyond which you emerge to the curve of **High Wray Bay**. The bridleway now veers away from the lake. The bay is a popular picnic spot, with people arriving both by land and by water. Walk the bikes round to the grassy slope above the further shore.

5 Retrace your route to Point 2.

6 A bridleway rises off to the right here. It offers the option of a direct route to the pub at **Far Sawrey**, but the climb is longer, steeper and rougher than what you have encountered so far – so unless you found that all too easy, it's best to ignore it and simply return to the **car park**. The road route to the pub requires riding for 1 mile (1.6km) on the **B5285**, which can be busy at times, and also involves a steep climb midway.

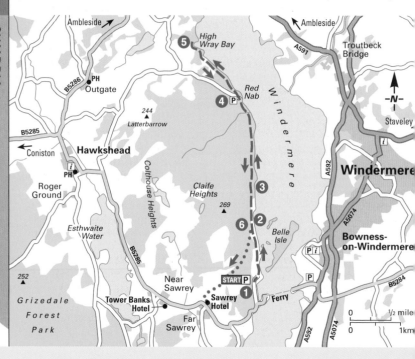

Sawrey Hotel

The Sawrey Hotel unites three original buildings into a remarkably harmonious whole. The oldest part, on the left of the current hotel entrance, dates back to around 1700. To the left again is the former stable block, altered in 1971 to form the Claife Crier Bar. This gets its name from a ghostly local legend, illustrated on the sign above the door. Some of the original stalls have been retained, making attractive and secluded seating areas, and the old beams are believed to have come from ships wrecked on the Cumbrian coast. Original horse-collars and other memorabilia decorate the walls. Outside is a pleasant garden, which keeps the sun until late in the evening and has views to Coniston Old Man and Swirl How.

Food

Bar lunches include smoked salmon sandwiches, a Hiker's lunch (cheddar cheese), smoked Esthwaite trout with salad, local venison sausage with tomato and apple chutney, and beef casserole. Set dinner menu only.

Family facilities

Children are welcome in the bar until 7pm, and allowed in the lounge at all times. At lunch, younger children have their own menu, and old children can chose smaller portions of some adult dishes. Safe garden.

Alternative refreshment stops

None along the route. The New Inn at Far Sawrey and Tower Banks Arms in Sawrey.

☞ Where to go from here

Hill Top is the 17th-century farmhouse at Near Sawrey where Beatrix Potter wrote and illustrated her tales of Peter Rabbit and his friends (tel 015394 36269; www.nationaltrust.org.uk).

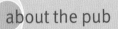

about the pub

Sawrey Hotel
Far Sawrey, Ambleside
Cumbria LA22 0LQ
Tel 015394 43425

DIRECTIONS: on the B5285	
PARKING: 30	
OPEN: daily, all day	
FOOD: daily lunchtime bar menu	
BREWERY/COMPANY: free house	
REAL ALE: Black Sheep Bitter, Theakston Best, Hawkshead Bitter, Jennings Cumberland Ale, guest beer	
ROOMS: 18 en suite	

Brant Fell at Bowness-on-Windermere

WALK

From Windermere's shores to high ground above the bustling town.

Bowness-on-Windermere

Fed by the high rainfall of the Lake District fells, via the rivers Brathay, Rothay and Troutbeck, Windermere is England's largest natural lake. It stretches some 12 miles

(19km) in length, is up to 1 mile (1.6km) wide in places, and reaches a depth of 220 feet (67m).

Bowness-on-Windermere is the main gateway and access point to the lake, and the most popular holiday destination in the Lake District. Over 10,000 boats for recreation are registered on the lake. The town developed rapidly after the Oxenholme and Kendal-to-Windermere

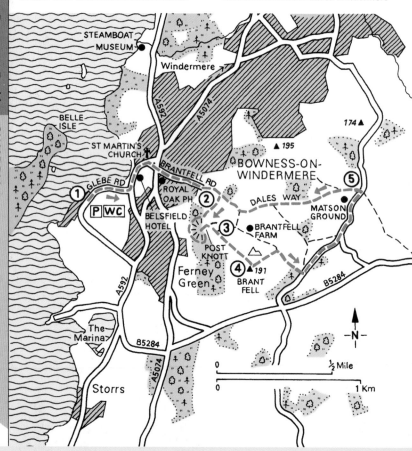

railway line opened in 1847, growing up around the station from the nucleus of what was once a small village. Indeed it was the railway company that named the station Windermere to attract a trade, although it is sited some distance from the lake. In the late 19th century wealthy businessmen, principally from the industrial towns of Lancashire, built large and luxurious residences overlooking the lake. Many of these private houses have been converted into hotels, such as the Langdale Chase, and Brockhole has been the National Park Visitor Centre since the late 1960s.

The Belsfield Hotel, overlooking Bowness Bay, was bought in 1860 by Henry Schneider, the chairman of the Barrow Steelworks and Shipworks. Reputedly he would leave his luxurious home and board his steam yacht SL *Esperance*, where he breakfasted while travelling across the lake to Lakeside. He would continue his journey to Barrow by steam train – he owned the railway and had his own private carriage.

the walk

1 Walk up **Glebe Road** (against the traffic) to the steamer pier. Cross the main road here and follow it left. Opposite the impressive **Church of St Martin** turn right to ascend the little street of **St Martin's Hill**. Cross the Kendal road to climb **Brantfell Road** directly above and pass the **Royal Oak Inn**. At the head of the road an iron gate leads on to the **Dales Way**, a stony path climbing directly up the hillside. Continue to a kissing gate by a wood.

A wet dock at the Steamboat Museum, Bowness-on-Windermere

1h30 — **3.5 MILES** — **5.7 KM** — **LEVEL 1 2 3**

WALK

Brant Fell CUMBRIA

MAP: OS Explorer OL 7 The English Lakes (SE)

START/FINISH: pay-and-display car park on Glebe Road above lake, Bowness-on-Windermere; grid ref: SD 398966

PATHS: pavement, road, stony tracks, grassy paths, 2 stiles

LANDSCAPE: town, mixed woodland, open fell, lake and fell views

PUBLIC TOILETS: at car park and above information centre

TOURIST INFORMATION: Windermere, tel 015394 46499

THE PUB: Royal Oak Inn, Bowness-on-Windermere, see Point **1** on route

⚠ Care needed with traffic on busy streets at the start and finish. Suitability: children 6+

Getting to the start
Bowness-on-Windermere is located on the A592 just south of Windermere town, and the A591 Kendal-to-Ambleside road. In Bowness, turn left just before the steamer terminal into Glebe Road, where the main car parks are located.

Researched and written by:
Bill Birkett, Jon Sparks

2 Pass through the kissing gate and turn right on a stony lane, signposted 'Post Knott'. Follow this up through the woods until it crests a rise near the flat, circular top of **Post Knott**. Bear left and make the final short ascent to the summit. The view from here was once exceptional but is now mainly obscured by trees. Retrace a few steps back to the track to find a **kissing gate** leading out of the wood on to the open hillside.

3 Take the path beyond the kissing gate, rising to a rocky shoulder. Cross the shoulder and bear left to a ladder stile near the top corner of the field between birch and holly trees. Immediately over the stile the path forks. Bear right to ascend directly up the open grassy flanks of **Brant Fell** to its rocky summit.

4 Bear left (north) from the highest point. The path is very indistinct but there are cairns, and the prominent white buildings of **Matson Ground** are a good guide. Go through a kissing gate into a new plantation. Emerge onto a stony track. Turn right and follow the track to a stone stile and gate, which lead on to the road. Turn left and continue left at the junction, to pass the stone buildings and entrance drive to Matson Ground. Just beyond is a kissing gate on the left, waymarked for the Dales Way.

Rowing boats beside a jetty onto Lake Windermere

what to look for

St Martin's Church, an impressive building surrounded by ancient yew trees, is the parish church of Bowness, built in 1483 and restored and enlarged in 1870. It is well worth taking a look inside. Behind the church is the oldest area of Bowness, known as Lowside, where an intriguing web of narrow streets thread between buildings of dark slate.

5 Go through the kissing gate. Then continue down the field to cross a track. Pass through another kissing gate. Follow the path, under the trees, to the left of a new **pond**, until it swings left to emerge through a kissing gate onto a surfaced drive. Go right along the drive for 30yds (27m) until the path veers off left through the trees to follow the fence. An **iron kissing gate** leads into a field. Follow the grassy path, first descending and then rising to an **iron gate** in the corner of the field. Go through it and follow the wall on the left to a kissing gate leading to a walled track. Cross the surfaced drive of **Brantfell Farm.** Keep straight on to another kissing gate leading to a field. Follow the path downhill, alongside the wall, to another kissing gate, with the stony lane of Point 2 just beyond. Retrace your steps back to **Glebe Road**.

26

WALK

Brant Fell CUMBRIA

Royal Oak Inn

about the pub

Royal Oak Inn
Brantfell Road,
Bowness-on-Windermere
Cumbria LA23 3EE
Tel 015394 43970

DIRECTIONS: close to St Martin's Church at the start of the walk
PARKING: very limited, so use walk car park
OPEN: daily, all day
FOOD: daily, all day
BREWERY/COMPANY: free house
REAL ALE: Coniston Bluebird, Tetley, Greene King Old Speckled Hen, guest beers
DOGS: not allowed indoors
ROOMS: 9 bedrooms

The Royal Oak is the official finishing pub for the Dales Way, so it seems fitting to make it the unofficial finishing pub for our much shorter walk. It's a tall slate building set back from the road, just off the bustling main street in slightly quieter surroundings, and a stone's throw from Bowness Bay piers and Windermere. As befits a pub that sets out to serve hungry walkers, it serves an extensive range of food throughout the day and quenches thirsts with handpumped ales, including the award-winning and locally brewed Coniston Bluebird.

Food

The pub specialises in griddled steaks with a choice of sauces, but also offers traditional fish and chips, chilli nachos, sandwiches and light snacks such as blue cheese and asparagus tart with red onion and tomato chutney.

Family facilities

Children are welcome in the left-hand side of the pub. There's a children's menu and on fine days the small garden at the front (away from the road) is the place to sit and eat.

Alternative refreshment stops

Bowness-on-Windermere is inundated with cafés, inns, shops and restaurants. Santameras Bakery Café is conveniently located near the start and finish of the route, at the foot of Brantfell Road.

☛ Where to go from here

The Windermere Steamboat Centre, 0.5 mile (800m) north of Bowness on the A592, has many working exhibits and provides a chance to chug across the lake on a genuine steam yacht, weather permitting (tel 015394 45565).

Around the Winster Valley from Bowland Bridge

A loop through a delightful secluded valley, with minimal traffic.

The Winster Valley

The valley floor and the hills to the west are of slate, the ridges to the east of limestone. The strata in both cases generally dip down towards the east, and the younger limestone actually lies on top of the older slate.

The slate is part of what geologists call the Windermere Group of rocks and is roughly 400 million years old. The limestone – carboniferous limestone, to be precise – is 300–350 million years old, and quite young by geological standards (the most ancient rocks in Britain are nearly ten times as old).

The woods on the western slopes of the valley are dominated by oak, while on the limestone ash trees are more common, with many gnarled yew trees on steeper slopes and where the soil is thin. You can see some fine examples where the lane climbs the steep flank of Yewbarrow. Yews are tough, slow-growing, long-lived trees and

able to survive where there seems to be hardly any soil. It is also worth knowing that yews are the best trees to shelter under when it rains, as their down-sloping leaves shed the water to the outside.

the ride

1 Follow the road, with the pub on your left, and cross the **bridge** that gives Bowland Bridge its name. Soon the road begins to climb quite steeply. Fortunately, you don't have to go too far up before you turn off to the left, signposted to Cartmel Fell and High Newton. There's a brief stretch of more level riding, then another short steep climb before you swoop down past the turning for **Cartmel Fell Church**. Continue straight on to meet a wider road at an angled junction.

2 Go straight across the junction on to a surfaced track over a cattle grid, signed to Ashes and Low Thorphinsty. Go through **Ashes farmyard**. After another 100yds (91m) the way ahead is blocked by

A cyclist negotiating a path lined with bushes and plants near Ashes in the Winster Valley

a gate. Turn left immediately before this, go through another gate and down a grassy track. After a second gate the grass gets longer, but it's only a short way further to a lane. While it's rarely muddy, the long grass will give you a good wetting after rain.

3 Turn right along the lane and follow it easily down the valley for 2 miles (3.2km) to a **crossroads** with an old-fashioned black-and-white **signpost**.

4 Turn left, signed to Witherslack. Climb slightly over the **Holme**, a slatey hump rising from the valley floor, then dip down again to **Bleacrag Bridge**. Bear left at the junction, at a triangle of grass, on to a narrow lane which has remnants of grass down the middle. This gradually draws closer to the rocky limestone flanks of Yewbarrow, climbing into a dark tunnel of yew trees. There are lots of exposed roots in the thin soil, and the first close glimpses of the limestone. Another lane joins in from the right.

The view south west across Winster Valley

1h30 — **9.5 MILES** — **15.3 KM** — **LEVEL 1 2**

MAP: OS Explorer OL 7 The English Lakes (SE)
START/FINISH: Bowland Bridge; grid ref: SD 417896
TRAILS/TRACKS: quiet lanes, with a short optional section on grassy bridleway
LANDSCAPE: lush valley overlooked by limestone escarpment
PUBLIC TOILETS: none on route
TOURIST INFORMATION: Bowness-on-Windermere, tel 015394 42895
CYCLE HIRE: South Lakeland Mountain Bike Sales & Hire, Lowick Bridge, Ulverston, tel 01229 885210; Wheelbase, Staveley, tel 01539 821443
THE PUB: Hare & Hounds Country Inn, Bowland Bridge, see Point **1** on route
🚲 Undulating ride with a few steep hills. Suitability: children 8+

(27)

🚲
CYCLE

Winster Valley

CUMBRIA

Getting to the start

Bowland Bridge is a tiny village 1.75 miles (2.8km) south west of Crossthwaite, on a minor road between the A5074 and the A592. Park in the small lay-by opposite the Hare & Hounds Country Inn, or in others scattered along the first part of the route.

Why do this cycle ride?

Although close to main roads and to tourist honeypots like Bowness, the Winster Valley is remarkably quiet. It's a great place for a relaxing ride, with few worries about traffic and a better than average chance of sunshine – for the Lake District. Limestone crags overlook the lush valley floor with its outcrops of slate, a geological boundary that marks a contrast between the earlier and later stages of the ride.

Researched and written by: Jon Sparks

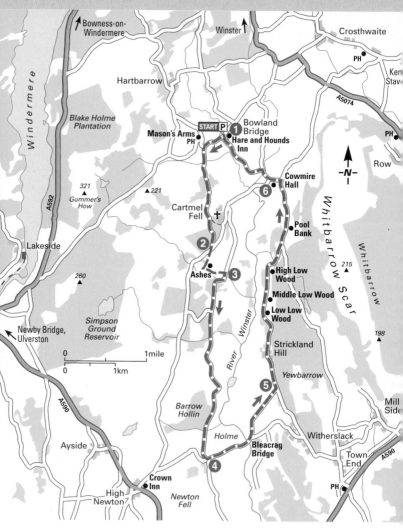

5 Continue along the lane past **Strickland Hill** and **Askew Green** until the way kinks through the farmyard of **Low Low Wood**, with a fine barn. Go through a gate ahead on to a rougher section of lane, past **Middle Low Wood** and **High Low Wood**. Climb to a T-junction and turn left. As you come over the crest and twist down past the beautiful **Pool Bank farm**, there's the best view yet of the steep flanks of the **Whitbarrow ridge**. At another grass triangle turn left, signed to Bowland Bridge.

6 Keep right past **Cowmire Hall**, swing round and drop down to another junction. Keep left here and go along the valley bottom near the river to reach the junction at **Bowland Bridge**. The **Hare and Hounds** is just to the right.

Hare & Hounds Country Inn

In the beautiful Winster Valley, with stunning views over Cartmel Fell, this 17th-century coaching inn is just 10 minutes' drive from the southern tip of Windermere. It's a truly rural, attractive building that successfully blends ancient and modern, with its rough stone walls, farming memorabilia and simple wooden furniture. Crackling log fires warm you in winter. On fine days head outside with your drinks and sit and survey the terrain covered by the ride. It's easy to overlook the orchard garden to the side of the pub, south-facing and enjoying views down the valley dominated by the crag-fringed ridge of Whitbarrow Scar. What better place to savour a pint from the ever-changing selection of real ales.

about the pub

Hare & Hounds Country Inn
Bowland Bridge, Grange-over-Sands
Cumbria LA11 6NN
Tel 015395 68333

DIRECTIONS: on the main road through the village

PARKING: 50

OPEN: closed Tuesday, open all day Saturday and Sunday

FOOD: daily

BREWERY/COMPANY: free house

REAL ALE: 4 changing guest beers

ROOMS: 3 en suite

Food

Satisfying bar meals include filled baps (Brie, bacon and cranberry), speciality Thai mussels with lemon grass, lime, chilli and fresh coriander, ploughman's lunches, fish pie and warm salads. Look to the seasonal menu for roast duck, shank of lamb, poached salmon and chargrilled steaks.

Family facilities

Children are welcome, and on summer days they can play on the swings in the garden.

Alternative refreshment stops

The Mason's Arms (great beer and super views) at top of Strawberry Bank near the start.

☛ Where to go from here

South east of Crossthwaite, Levens Hall is a fascinating Elizabethan house, noted for its plasterwork, panelling and topiary garden (tel 015395 60321).

Over Hampsfell from Grange-over-Sands

A walk through woods and over open fell above a charming seaside resort.

Grange-over-Sands
TAKE NOTICE
All persons visiting this Hospice by permission of the owner, are requested to respect private property, and not by acts of wanton mischief and destruction show that they possess more muscle than brain. I have no hope that this request will be attended to...
G Remington

So reads one of the panels inside the peculiar Hospice of Hampsfell at the high point of this walk. Its tone matches that of Grange-over-Sands, with its neat and tidy white limestone buildings, colourful gardens, sunny aspect and seaside disposition. It has long been a popular seaside resort, particularly since the Furness Railway reached the town in 1857. Day trippers also arrived by steamer across Morecambe Bay, disembarking at the Claire House Pier, which was dramatically blown away by a storm in 1928.

Today the sea is somewhat distanced from the sea wall, and the town, bypassed by mainstream holidaymakers, retains a refined air of quiet dignity. Grange has many splendid buildings and its ornamental gardens, complete with ponds, are a good place to relax and enjoy a picnic. The gardens rise to the open airy spaces of Hampsfell (Hampsfield Fell on the map) via the mixed woodland of Eggerslack.

The neat square tower, around 20ft (6m) high, which adorns the top of Hampsfield Fell, is known as the Hospice of Hampsfell. It was apparently built by a minister from nearby Cartmel Priory over a century ago for 'the shelter and entertainment of travellers over the fell'. Enclosed by a fence of chains to keep cattle out, it provides a convenient shelter should the weather take a turn for the worse. On its north face stone steps give access to the top of the tower and a fabulous view. On the top, a novel direction indicator, which consists of a wooden sighting arrow mounted on a rotating circular table, lets you know which distant point of interest you are looking at. Simply align the arrow to the chosen subject, read the angle created by the arrow and locate it on the list on the east rail.

the walk

1 From the north end of the car park walk through the **ornamental gardens**. The most direct route keeps left, close to the main road. Exit to the mini-roundabout and take the road signed to Newby Bridge, Ulverston, Windermere. Go up and round the bend, and find steps up to a **squeeze stile** on the left, signed 'Routen Well/Hampsfield'.

2 Take the path rising through **Eggerslack Wood**. Cross directly over a surfaced track and continue, to pass a house on the left. Steps lead on to a track. Cross this diagonally to follow a track, signed '**Hampsfell**'. The track makes one zig-zag and then climbs directly through the woods, passing old reservoirs which once supplied water to one of the hotels. At the top is a wall and stile.

what to look for

Rising skyward above the main street and below the church, the clock tower is noted as one of the finest buildings in Grange. It was financed by Mrs Sophia Deardon and built in 1912 from local limestone (probably from the quarry at Eden Mount) and the chocolate-brown St Bees sandstone.

If you look up the Fell Road out of Grange you will see an impressive white limestone building. Hardcragg Hall is the oldest house in Grange and is dated 1563. John Wilkinson, ironmaster, once lived here. His first iron boat was launched some 2 miles (3.2km) away at Castlehead on the River Winster.

3 Cross the stile and follow the signposted path up the open hillside, passing sections of limestone pavement and little craggy outcrops. Cross another stile and go right along the wall. Where it veers away, continue in the same direction, following a grassy track past ancient stone cairns to the tower landmark of the **Hospice of Hampsfell**.

4 Turn left at the tower and follow the path over the edge of a little limestone escarpment (slippery rock). Continue over another escarpment and gently down to a stile. Keep straight ahead through a dip and up the green hill beyond. Cross over

Gardens and ornamental lake at Grange-over-Sands, the start point of the walk

Hampsfell CUMBRIA

2h00 — **4 MILES** — **6.4 KM** — **LEVEL 2**

MAP: OS Explorer OL 7 The English Lakes (SE)

START/FINISH: car park below road and tourist office, central Grange; grid ref: SD 410780

PATHS: paths and tracks, can be muddy in places, 7 stiles

LANDSCAPE: town, woods and open fell, extensive seascapes

PUBLIC TOILETS: at Ornamental Gardens, north end of car park

TOURIST INFORMATION: Grange-over-Sands, tel 015395 34026

THE PUB: The Lancastrian, Grange-over-Sands, near the start of the route

🛑 Care needed with traffic on busy streets at the start and finish. Suitability: children 6+

Getting to the start

Grange-over-Sands is on the coast, south of Newby Bridge. Take the B5277 into the town. Just after the railway station keep left and follow the main street until signs point to a parking area down a lane on the left, below the Commodore Inn.

Researched and written by:
Bill Birkett, Jon Sparks

the top and descend again to a gate and stile. Although the path bears left here, it is usual to continue directly to the little cairn on **Fell End**, with fine views over **Morecambe Bay**. Go sharp left to rejoin the main path, which skirts to the left of a little valley of thorn bushes and descends to a gate and a road.

5 Cross the road, take the squeeze stile and descend diagonally left across the field to a gate on to a road by the front door of **Springbank Cottage**. Descend the surfaced track to enter a farmyard and bear right to a **stone stile**. Go over the hill, following the path parallel to the wall and

cross a stile into a narrow path. Follow this, with a high wall to the right, round the corner and down to a road junction. Go left on a private road/public footpath, and then bear right at the fork. At the next junction turn right to descend the track and at the following junction go left down **Charney Well Lane**. When you get to another junction, bear left below the woods of **Eden Mount**. Keep descending to a T-junction and go right. At the junction with a larger road go left (toilets to the right) and descend past the church and clock tower to a junction with the main road (**B5277**). Go left and then right to the **car park**.

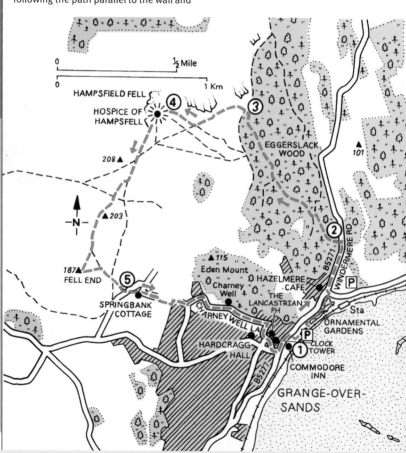

The Lancastrian

The Lancastrian is just a minute or two off the direct route of the walk, and occupies part of what used to be the town's cinema and dance hall. Inside the decor is, by and large, 'pubby' enough, but look for various literary quotations inscribed on the beams.

Food
Typical main dishes include chunky shepherd's pie, neck of lamb, scrumpy pork hock and duck breast in plum and ginger sauce. Lighter snacks include sandwiches and ploughman's lunches.

Family facilities
Children under supervision are welcome in the bars. Outdoor seating is limited to a couple of pavement tables.

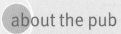
about the pub

The Lancastrian
Main Street, Grange-over-Sands
Cumbria LA11 6AB
Tel 015395 32455

DIRECTIONS: just off the walk – look up to the right from the mini-roundabout by the clock tower

PARKING: use walk car park

OPEN: daily, all day

FOOD: no food Tuesday

BREWERY/COMPANY: free house

REAL ALE: Boddingtons, Castle Eden Ale, guest beer

DOGS: welcome inside

WALK

Hampsfell

CUMBRIA

Alternative refreshment stops
Grange-over-Sands has many excellent cafés and inns catering for a wide range of tastes. On the route, of particular merit are the Commodore Inn and Hazelmere Café.

☛ Where to go from here
North of Newby Bridge at Lakeside, on the southern tip of Windermere, is the Aquarium of the Lakes, home to the UK's largest collection of freshwater fish and with a series of themed natural habitats (www.aquariumofthelakes.co.uk).

Across Heughscar Hill from Pooley Bridge

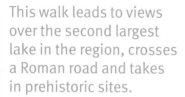

This walk leads to views over the second largest lake in the region, crosses a Roman road and takes in prehistoric sites.

Romans and ancients

The walk takes in a short section of the High Street, a Roman road. This leads directly to the Cockpit stone circle which, although not a circle of upright standing stones, is quite distinct and unmistakable. Two concentric stone circles, some standing, some fallen, contain a circular bank of earth and stones up to 3ft (1m) high. It has an internal radius of around 85ft (26m) and, as it is thought to be of Bronze Age origin, c2000 BC, it predates the Roman road. In more recent times, it was used as an arena for cockfighting, a once-popular sport that was outlawed in 1849.

Extending south east from here is desolate Moor Divock where many prehistoric burial mounds and cairns are hidden in the landscape of coarse hill grass, bracken, heather and bog. A mound known as White Raise, presumably because of the white quartz which marks its rocks, was partially excavated in the 19th century. A crouched skeleton was revealed in one of its cists (a coffin or burial chamber of stone or wood). Near by, the Cop Stone, a gnarled standing stone some 5ft (1.6m) high, tops a low hill and provides a direction indicator in this otherwise rather featureless landscape. Local sports were held by this stone up until 1800, and tradition claims that an avenue of standing stones known as the Shap Avenue once

led to it. Two further Bronze Age stone circles close by, referred to as Moor Divock 4 and Moor Divock 5, have been partially excavated to reveal urns and ashes.

the walk

1 From the bridge crossing the **River Eamont** follow the main street **(B5320)** through the centre of Pooley Bridge. Pass **The Sun Inn** and the **church,** then turn right to follow the pavement along the Howtown road.

2 At the junction continue over the crossroads. The road (**Roe Head Lane**) rises pleasantly through trees, ending at an unsurfaced track beneath **Roehead**. A gate and kissing gate lead out on to the open moor.

3 Climb the broad track beyond the gate. Just before it levels out, at a **cairn,** a recently resurfaced track bears off to the right.

A wintery view over Ullswater from Hallin Fell

2h00 — **4.5 MILES** — **7.2 KM** — **LEVEL 1 2 3**

MAP: OS Explorer OL 5 The English Lakes (NE)

START/FINISH: pay-and-display car parks either side of the bridge, Pooley Bridge; grid ref: NY 470244

PATHS: surfaced roads, stony tracks, grassy tracks and hillside

LANDSCAPE: village, dale and open fell

PUBLIC TOILETS: centre of Pooley Bridge

TOURIST INFORMATION: Pooley Bridge, tel 017684 86530

THE PUB: The Sun Inn, Pooley Bridge, see Point **1** on route

🛑 Navigation can be tricky on upper reaches of Heughscar Hill in poor visibility.
Suitability: children 6+

Pooley Bridge CUMBRIA

Getting to the start
Pooley Bridge lies at the top of Ullswater. From the M6, junction 40, head west on the A66 for 1 mile (1.6km). Turn left on the A592 for 3.5 miles (5.7km), then turn left on the B5320 into the village. There are car parks both before and after the bridge.

Researched and written by:
Bill Birkett, Jon Sparks

4 Follow the clear track, on the line of the **High Street** Roman road, to reach an ancient, low circular wall of earth and stone. This is **the Cockpit**, the largest of the many prehistoric antiquities found on **Moor Divock**.

5 Turn left on another reconstructed track, curving to the left at a marshy dip. Pass some shallow shake holes (sinkholes) before crossing the original track at **Ketley Gate** (there's no actual gate here). A little to the right is **White Raise** burial cairn. Follow the track ahead towards a walled wood high on the hillside. As the track begins to level, bear left to the top corner of the wood. Turn left on a grassy track and then bear right on a narrower track parting the bracken, to the cairn on the highest point of **Heughscar Hill**. This is in a commanding position offering extensive views.

Pooley Bridge

CUMBRIA

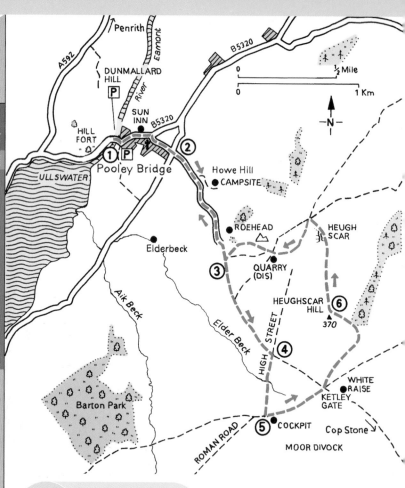

what to look for

The High Street Roman road is followed for two short sections of this walk. In its full length, the road traverses the eastern Lakeland fells, exceeding a height of 2,500ft (762m) in several places. It stretches from the Troutbeck Valley near Ambleside to Brougham by the River Eamont, where it intercepts the main south east/north west Roman arterial road. Even today, though heavily eroded in places, it remains a remarkable testament to the ambition of Roman engineering.

6 Bear right on a broad green track, to pass the broken limestone crag of **Heugh Scar** below to the left. At the end of the scar a faint path descends the steep hillside to the well-worn **High Street**. Turn left on this for 300yds (274m), then bear right on a green track towards the corner of a stone wall at the top of a line of trees. Just before reaching this, pass a small quarry and the remains of a lime kiln. From the wall corner descend steeply alongside the wall until the track of the outward leg comes into view. Bear left to regain it and turn right. Retrace the outward route back to **Pooley Bridge**.

The Sun Inn

The 18th-century Sun Inn presents a classic Lakeland pub frontage, white with black trim, and brightened with plenty of colourful hanging baskets in summer. The interior retains much of its original character, with some fine wood panelling, open log fires, and low-beamed ceilings throughout the rambling and intimate bars and dining room. Real ales are from the Jennings Brewery in Cockermouth – relax by the crackling log fire and sup a pint of the strong and dark Sneck Lifter after walking this route on a bracing winter's day.

about the pub

The Sun Inn
Pooley Bridge, Penrith
Cumbria CA10 2NN
Tel 017684 86205
www.suninnpooleybridge.co.uk

DIRECTIONS: in the village centre, diagonally opposite the church	
PARKING: 50	
OPEN: daily, all day	
FOOD: daily	
BREWERY/COMPANY: Jennings Brewery	
REAL ALE: Jennings Bitter, Cumberland Ale and Sneck Lifter	
DOGS: welcome inside	
ROOMS: 9 en suite	

Food
At lunchtime tuck into a range of sandwiches, filled jacket potatoes and traditional pub snacks. For something more substantial, order braised lamb Jennings, home-made chilli, vegetable Kiev, or the hearty fellman's salad.

Family facilities
The welcome and provision for families is good, with children allowed inside. Smaller portions of certain main dishes are available and there are baby-changing facilities in the toilets. The large garden is backed by mature trees with great views over fields to the surrounding fells.

Alternative refreshment stops
Numerous cafés and inns in the village of Pooley Bridge cater for a wide range of tastes.

☛ Where to go from here
Take a boat trip on Ullswater. Two beautifully preserved 19th-century boats, *Lady of the Lake* and *Raven*, run regular trips from the jetty at Pooley Bridge, stopping at the landing stages at Howtown and Glenridding.

Around Askham and Bampton

CYCLE

Askham CUMBRIA

A pleasing loop, rich in ancient hedgerows and fine open scenery.

Fabulous flora

This is a great ride for wildflower-spotting as the low altitude and sunny aspect conspire with the limestone-based soils to produce a wide variety of blooms along the waysides. The lane up the east side of the valley, after Bampton Grange, is particularly rewarding. The hedges along the initial section are full of white hawthorn blossom in May and dog-roses in June. After the main climb on this section there are some fine flowery banks along the lane, with masses of cow parsley and some impressive sweeps of reddish-purple bloody cranesbill, a species of geranium. The name 'cranesbill' comes from the shape of its seed-pods.

A little further on, pause on Crookwath bridge to look down on the streamers of water crowfoot, an aquatic type of buttercup, with white flowers in early summer. Most of the trees along the banks are alder. Alder is happy growing 'with its feet in the water', and the wood it yields

is remarkably water-resistant. (The city of Venice is largely built on alderwood piles.)

the ride

1 From the **car park** follow the main road south through the village, dog-legging past the **The Queens Head** pub, with the greens stretching off to left and right. Keep on along this road, enjoying the generally easy gradients and views down the valley ahead to the **Shap Fells**. Across the valley on the left is the sharp profile of **Knipe Scar**.

2 After just over 1 mile (1.6km), on the boundary of **Helton**, branch off right on a loop road through the village. The extra climb is worth it for the pretty cottages and flowery verges. Ease back down to rejoin the valley road and continue, with a network of limestone walls and small fields flanking the road on the right. As the road starts to descend, two lanes branch off to the right from a shared junction.

Fell ponies grazing in fields above Heltondale with Beck and Knipe Scar on the skyline

A limestone wall and dog-rose bush on a lane near Bampton Grange

3 Take the left-hand lane and follow it for 400yds (366m) to a cattle grid, for a look at the **old mill**, with an overgrown watercourse, on **Heltondale Beck**. Continue a little further until the lane reaches open fell. There are good views here and you may sometimes find fell ponies grazing. Retrace to the road at Point 3 and turn right to continue, now descending. At the bottom swing right over **Beckfoot Bridge** and continue along the level valley floor, passing another collection of pretty cottages at **Butterwick**. Note that the walls here have changed from silvery limestone to greyer Lakeland rock. Climb a little before reaching the outskirts of **Bampton**, then go down into the village.

4 The post office and village shop (open long hours) has a café attached, information panels on the wall and more information inside. Over the bridge opposite the shop, it's just a short way up the lane to the pretty **Mardale Inn**. (Those looking for a longer ride could continue up this lane for 2 miles/3.2km to **Naddle Bridge** and **Haweswater**.) Continue along the main valley road towards **Bampton Grange**, swinging left into the village over a bridge crossing the **River Lowther**, and past the **Crown and Mitre** pub.

5 On the edge of the village, turn left, signposted 'Knipe, Whale'. Look back to the left over **Bampton Grange**, with the fells behind rising to the great smooth ridges along which the Romans built their road now known as **High Street**. Cross a

1h15 | **9 MILES** | **14.2 KM** | **LEVEL 1** 23

MAP: OS Explorer OL 5 The English Lakes (NE)

START/FINISH: village car park, Askham; grid ref: NY 513237

TRAILS/TRACKS: quiet lanes

LANDSCAPE: open valley with pasture and woodland, views to higher fells

PUBLIC TOILETS: none on route

TOURIST INFORMATION: Penrith, tel 01768 867466

CYCLE HIRE: Keswick Mountain Bikes, tel 017687 75202

THE PUB: The Queens Head, Askham, see Point **1** on route

 Few steep climbs and descents. Suitability: children 8+

Getting to the start

Askham is south of Penrith and the M6, junction 40. From there, take the A66 east. Turn right on the A6, go through Eamont Bridge, then turn right on the B5320. Go over a railway bridge, then turn left to reach Askham. There is a signposted car park on the left as you enter the village.

Why do this cycle ride?

The valley of the River Lowther runs south from Askham. Delightful on a fine day, it may also escape the worst of the weather when it's raining, as it lies in the 'rain shadow' of the Lakeland fells. This pleasant road circuit has few steep gradients and is away from the main tourist routes.

Researched and written by: Jon Sparks

cattle grid on to open fell. Look up to the right to the low crags of **Knipe Scar**. The lane climbs gently, with great views of the valley and the fells to the west. Descend to a junction by a **phone box** and turn right through a gate. Climb quite steeply to another gate, beyond which the road continues to climb more gradually. The going levels off for a stretch before beginning to descend. Whizz back down into the valley, keeping straight on at a junction, and down to the river at **Crookwath Bridge**.

6 The climb away from the river is gentle but quite sustained, levelling off just before a T-junction. Emerge with care as some traffic moves quite fast here, and go right, almost immediately back into **Askham**.

A s k h a m CUMBRIA

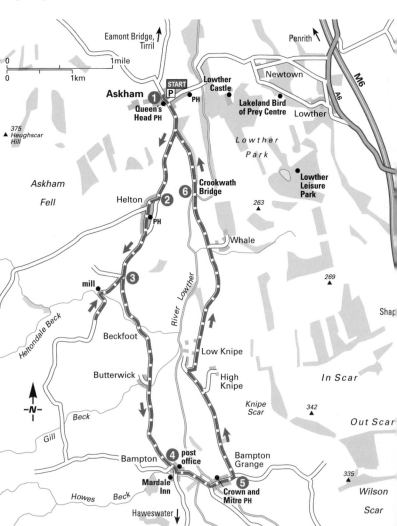

The Queens Head

A picture-book village complete with river, church and castle is the lovely setting for this popular late 17th-century pub. Lowther Castle is just a few minutes' walk away. The bar has low ceilings, horse-brasses, copper kettles and some stuffed animal heads, but the best features are the old fireplace (dated 1682) and the wall cupboard alongside, dated 1698. There is also a rambling, beamed lounge, roaring log fires and a games room with pool and darts. Outdoor seating is limited to two small paved areas, and the front benches overlook the village green.

about the pub

The Queens Head
Askham, Penrith
Cumbria CA10 8PF
Tel 01931 712225

DIRECTIONS: in the centre of Askham, near Lowther Castle	
PARKING: 8 (village car park adjacent)	
OPEN: daily, all day in summer	
FOOD: daily	
BREWERY/COMPANY: Vaux Brewery	
REAL ALE: Tetley, guest beer	
ROOMS: 4 en suite	

Food
Along with a range of curries, salads, cold and hot baguettes and burgers, the menu offers Cumberland sausage, steak and onion pie, braised Lakeland lamb with minted gravy, and broccoli, Stilton and walnut crumble. Separate restaurant menu.

Family facilities
Children are welcome inside the pub, and younger family members have their own menu.

Alternative refreshment stops
The Punchbowl in Askham, café and the Mardale Inn at Bampton, and the Crown and Mitre in Bampton Grange.

☛ Where to go from here
Rheged, at Redhills, near Penrith, is named after Cumbria's Celtic kingdom, and is a state-of-the-art attraction buried under a man-made hill, complete with a huge cinema screen and a mountaineering exhibition (www.rheged.com).

The Eden Valley from Armathwaite

CYCLE

Discover an unsung but lovely corner, with exciting off-road options.

The Eden Valley

The route offers great views of both the Lake District and the Pennines, the latter being particularly well seen on the final descent. The highest peak is Cross Fell. At 2,930ft (893m) it is the highest peak in the Pennines and indeed the highest in England outside the Lake District, but is merely part of a massive mountain wall that hems in the Eden Valley to the east. It has a major influence on local weather and has its very own wind, the notorious Helm wind, possibly so called because it is accompanied by a helmet-like cap of cloud on the ridge.

The railway line which is crossed several times on the right – at track level if you take the first off-road option – is the Settle to Carlisle line, one of Britain's most scenic rail routes. It runs for 72 miles (116km) between Settle in North Yorkshire and Carlisle. Completed in 1876, the line was a major engineering challenge, with 20 viaducts and 14 tunnels. Its highest point is at Ais Gill summit, 1,169ft (356m) above sea level, and its most famous feature is probably the great Ribblehead viaduct, a few miles further south. It was the expense of restoring this, as well as general maintenance of the route, that led to a threat of closure in the 1990s, but a vigorous public campaign and the promotion of the line as a tourist attraction ensured its survival.

Top right: Railway viaduct near Armathwaite
Right: A cyclist using an unmanned crossing over the Settle to Carlisle rail line

the ride

1 Head north through the village and past the church, ignoring all turnings to right and left. Continue along this lane, with a few minor undulations before a dip alongside a railway viaduct. Now climb, in two stages, to the level crossing at **Lowhouse Crossing**. Bump across the line and continue less steeply to a junction near **Froddle Crook**. The old, rusty signpost has lost one arm.

2 For the shorter ride, turn left here and follow the lane beside **High Stand Plantation**, with fine views, to the crossroads at **Blackmoss Pool**. Go straight across to rejoin the longer route. For the longer route, go straight ahead at Froddle Crook for 1.5 miles (2.4km) to a turning on the left signed to Cotehill.

3 To stay on tarmac turn left here and follow the road for 1 mile (1.6km) to the crossroads in **Cotehill village**, then turn left. For the off-road alternative, continue straight ahead to a bridge over the railway

and then past a small **wood** on the left. At the end of the wood follow a bridleway sign left through a gate and down a short track. Where this bends left into a farmyard go straight ahead, through an awkward gate, and follow field edges, with no real track but no great difficulty unless the grass is high. At the bottom of the second field, just below the railway line, bear right on a short track to a gate and out onto the tracks. Cross with care – there is good visibility both ways. Go through the gate on the other side and straight out along a green track, rounding a bend to reach a clearer track. Follow this more easily, to emerge onto a road. Turn left for a short climb into **Cotehill**. Be alert where the road squeezes between two houses. At a crossroads, go straight across to rejoin the road alternative.

4 Carry straight on, signed to Armathwaite. Climb to **Stand End**, then on beside **High Stand Plantation** to the crossroads at **Blackmoss Pool** (more marsh than open water).

5 Turn right, signed to Aiketgate and Low Hesket. The tree-lined lane runs dead straight, first down, then up. A view of the fells opens up as the road dips to a T-junction. Turn left, signed to Nunclose and Armathwaite, and make a short climb into the hamlet of **Aiketgate**. A fork in the road, opposite the phone box, offers another off-road option.

6 To stay on tarmac, keep right here, and then bear left at the next fork. The lane begins a fine sweeping descent and the off-road alternative rejoins halfway down,

1h30	10 MILES	16.1 KM	LEVEL 1 2 3

LONGER ROUTE (OFF ROAD)

2h00	11 MILES	17.7 KM	LEVEL 1 2 3

SHORTER ALTERNATIVE ROUTE

1h00	6.5 MILES	10.4 KM	LEVEL 1 2 3

MAP: OS Explorer OL5 The English Lakes (NE) and OL315 Carlisle

START/FINISH: Armathwaite village; grid ref: NY 504461

TRAILS/TRACKS: lanes, with two optional off-road sections

LANDSCAPE: rolling farmland, woodland and river valley, views to distant fells

PUBLIC TOILETS: none on route

TOURIST INFORMATION: Carlisle, tel: 01228 625600

CYCLE HIRE: Scotby Cycles, Carlisle, tel 01228 546931

THE PUB: The Duke's Head, Armathwaite

🅛 Crosses rail tracks twice. The shorter road route is suitable for children 8+; the longer loop is for children 10+. Two optional off-road sections: the first is suitable for most abilities, the second is rougher and steeper, for experienced children 12+ only, mountain bike recommended. .

How to get to the start
Armathwaite east of Low Heskett and High Heskett, off the A6. There is no car park, so park considerately on verges.

Why do this cycle ride?
One of the unsung jewels of England, the Eden Valley retains a peaceful atmosphere that can be missing in the Lake District.

Researched and written by: Jon Sparks

Eden Valley

CUMBRIA

at **Windy Nook**. For the off-road adventure, take the left fork at Point 6. The tarmac lane leads into a stonier track, climbing steeply at first. The gradient eases, but the track continues stony all the way to the crest. The descent ahead is on a much greener track. This isn't difficult, just a little bumpy, but in summer the vegetation makes it hard to see where your wheels are going. Go through a gate and continue downhill, gradually curving right. The undergrowth

diminishes as the descent steepens. The final 100yds (91m) before the road are steep and tricky, with large stones and no soft landings: consider walking here. Rejoin the road at **Windy Nook** and turn left.

Continue on this road past the turning for Nunclose. The road swings round towards another railway viaduct. Keep left at another junction, go under the railway, and follow the road back into **Armathwaite**.

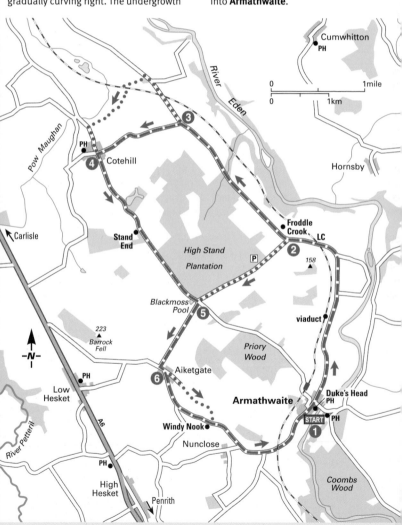

The Duke's Head

A long-standing favourite in the area, the comfortable, stone-built Duke's Head stays firmly traditional. Its fishing connections are well documented in the Last Cast Lounge, from where it's only a few paces into a glorious garden with flower beds and beech trees disappearing down the banks of the River Eden below. Fishing can be arranged for guests, who come here in search of the finest trout and salmon in the north of England. Expect stone walls, open log fires, oak tables and settles in the civilised lounge bar, a lively locals' bar dispensing tip-top Jennings bitter, and simply furnished bedrooms. The inn's bold claim to be the 'home of probably the best roast duck in Cumbria' is one which many will feel obliged to put to the test. Cyclists exploring the valley are made very welcome, and the pub even has some bikes for hire.

Food

Fresh local produce features on the wide-ranging menu. If you don't fancy roast duck, try hot potted Solway shrimps, venison steak with red wine, mushroom and redcurrant sauce, locally smoked salmon or prime steaks from a local farm. Or there are sandwiches and a 3-cheese platter.

about the pub

The Duke's Head
Armathwaite, Carlisle
Cumbria CA4 9PB
Tel 016974 72226

DIRECTIONS: From the A6 take the Armathwaite turning
PARKING: 40
OPEN: daily, all day
FOOD: daily
BREWERY/COMPANY: Punch Taverns
REAL ALE: Jennings Cumberland Ale, guest beers
ROOMS: 5 bedrooms (3 en suite)

Family facilities

Small portions from the main menu are available to children, who are welcome inside the pub. It's a super garden for summer alfresco eating and drinking, but beware the river.

Alternative refreshment stops

None on route but you'll also find the Fox and Pheasant by the river in Armathwaite.

☞ Where to go from here

Long Meg and Her Daughters is a Bronze Age stone circle at Little Salkeld, south of Kirkoswald (open access).

Kendal's two castles

WALK

Visit two ancient castles, on opposite banks of the River Kent.

Kendal

Characterful Kendal is known as the 'Auld Grey Town' for the colour of its predominantly limestone buildings. Sited either side of the River Kent, it has been occupied since Roman times, and its varied nooks, crannies and castles offer a rich historical tapestry.

Ruined Kendal Castle, in a commanding position above the town and the River Kent, is quietly impressive. The people of Kendal know it as an old friend, and may tell you that here was the birthplace of Catherine Parr who became Henry VIII's sixth and last wife in 1543. Although her grandfather, William Parr who died in 1483, lies entombed in Kendal parish church, apparently there is no evidence that Catherine ever set foot in Kendal and the castle was probably falling into decay by that time.

Kendal

CUMBRIA

Kendal Castle succeeded the older wooden, traditional motte and bailey Castle Howe – now reduced to a mound – on the opposite riverbank during the 12th century. Work started on Kendal's new castle in about 1220 and continued until 1280. Today, the ruins consist of a circular defensive wall and three towers, plus a residential gatehouse surrounded by a partly filled ditch.

The Parr family occupied the castle for four generations, from 1380 to 1486, when William Parr's widow remarried and moved to Northamptonshire. The castle's demise took place at a pace after this and much of the stone is thought to have been recycled for use in building works in the Auld Grey Town below.

the walk

1 Emerge on to the Kirkland Road, the main road through Kendal, and pass the **Ring O'Bells Inn** and the impressive iron gates of the church. Turn right along the road and proceed for 300yds (274m) to a crossing. Cross it, then continue up the main road. Cross **Gillingate Road**; the main road is now called **Highgate**. At Lightfoot's chemist shop go left up **Captain French Lane** for 300yds (274m), then go right up **Garth Heads**. Follow this to a flight of steps ascending to the left. More steps lead to a terrace and a view out over Kendal. Cross the grass terrace towards the mound and its distinct bodkin-shaped obelisk. Climb the steps and then spiral left until, as the path levels, steps lead up right to the obelisk and the top of **Castle Howe**.

The ruins of Kendal Castle, family home of Catherine Parr, Henry VIII's sixth wife

1h30 — 3 MILES — 4.8 KM — LEVEL 1 2 3

MAP: OS Explorer OL 7 The English Lakes (SE)

START/FINISH: car parks off Kirkland Road, Kendal; grid ref: SD 516921

PATHS: pavements, surfaced and grassy paths with steps, no stiles

LANDSCAPE: historic Kendal and open hillside

PUBLIC TOILETS: at car park above Abbot Hall Art Gallery, and near Miller Bridge

TOURIST INFORMATION: Kendal, tel 01539 725758

THE PUB: The Castle Inn, Kendal, near Point **3** on route

🛈 Care needed with traffic on busy streets. Suitability: children 6+

Getting to the start

Follow the A6 into the centre of Kendal and as it becomes one-way, get into the right-hand lane and turn into a car park on the right by the parish church. There's another small car park a little further on, round the S-bend in Kirkland.

Researched and written by: Bill Birkett, Jon Sparks

Kendal CUMBRIA

2 Return to the path and go right. Find a gap on the left and emerge onto the road (the top of **Beast Banks**). Descend the hill, which becomes **Allhallows Lane**, to the traffic lights and pedestrian crossing diagonally opposite the **Town Hall**. Cross the main road and go down **Lowther Street** to reach the river near **Miller Bridge**. Bear left and cross the road by the bridge; a car park and toilets are just beyond.

3 Walk upstream along the riverside parking area to a footbridge crossing the river. Cross and bear left to follow the

Kendal Castle

surfaced walkway, through **Gooseholme**. At the junction of roads by the **Church of St George** turn right down **Castle Street**. Pass The Castle Inn and continue up the hill to **Castle Road** on the right. Ascend **Castle Road** until a kissing gate on the right leads on to open, grassy **Castle Hill**. Follow the broad path ascending the shoulder to the ruins of **Kendal Castle**.

4 Go round the right (west) side of the castle ruins. Where the path forks, go right. After about a hundred paces drop down right on a narrow path with a railing. Pass through an iron kissing gate on to **Sunnyside Road**. Follow Sunnyside, which becomes **Parr Street**, and exit on to **Aynam Road**.

5 Turn right along Aynam Road to a crossing. Cross the road and the footbridge over the **River Kent**. Over the river turn left, downstream, for 250yds (229m). Turn right at a magnificent beech tree and limestone pillar onto a path lined by yew trees, to pass between **Kendal parish church** and **Abbot Hall Art Gallery**. The **car park** is just to the left.

what to look for

Castle Howe, Kendal's first Norman castle, was built between 1068 and 1100. At the time it was the cutting northern edge of the rapidly established Norman kingdom. Kendal, then known as Kirkbie Strickland, was mentioned in the Domesday survey of 1086. The obelisk on top of Castle Howe was designed by Francis Webster and built by William Holme in 1778. It was dedicated to the 'Glorious Revolution' of 1688 when William of Orange replaced James II. It is known locally as 'Bill Holmes' bodkin'.

The Castle Inn

about the pub

The Castle Inn
Castle Street, Kendal
Cumbria LA9 7AA
Tel 01539 729983

DIRECTIONS: on the east side of the river, just south of the railway station
PARKING: use town car parks
OPEN: daily, all day
FOOD: daily, lunchtimes only
BREWERY/COMPANY: Tetley
REAL ALE: Tetley, Jennings Bitter, guest beers
DOGS: welcome inside

It's already a two-castle walk, so it seems fitting to add a third in the shape of The Castle Inn. It stands tucked away in a haven of relative calm, out of the bustle of the town centre and just before you start to climb up to Kendal Castle. It is one of the oldest pubs in Kendal, recorded as being a beer house in 1834 and a thriving inn in about 1870. There are two rooms, both served by a central brass-railed bar. The comfortable lounge is quite small, while the public bar is a little more spacious and has an original Duttons Brewery window. But choosing between them may be a matter of which variety of entertainment you prefer: TV and pool table in the bar, or tropical fish tank and comfortable seating in the lounge. Do note before you set off that food is available only at lunchtimes.

Food
Good value lunches range from steak and onion sandwich, Cumberland sausage and egg and ploughman's lunches, to Castle Inn specials like giant Yorkshire puddings filled with steak and kidney, fresh haddock in light crispy batter, and home-made curries. Sunday roasts.

Family facilities
Families with children are welcome until 6pm. There's a standard children's menu and the impressive fish tank should keep younger children amused. Good games area for older children, and outdoor seating on the front pavement.

Alternative refreshment stops
Kendal is famed for its fine pubs and there is a plethora of cafés and restaurants. Try the Ring O'Bells or Ye Olde Fleece Inn, just up from the Town Hall. The Brewery Arts Centre, just beyond Captain French Lane along Highgate, has café and bar facilities.

☞ Where to go from here
Kendal Museum is just one of the attractions in the town, with everything from stuffed bears and crocodiles to Neolithic Langdale stone axes and a display about author Alfred Wainwright (www.kendalmuseum.org).

Talkin Tarn and the end of the Pennines

CYCLE

33

Talkin Tarn

CUMBRIA

A varied lane circuit from Talkin Tarn with some expansive views.

Talkin Tarn

Talkin Tarn appears to sit on a shelf on the hillside rather than in a valley. It is around 0.5 mile (800m) long, and big enough to be of value to rowers and scullers, as well as attracting a variety of waders and wildfowl. There is a legend that a drowned village lies at the bottom of the lake, still visible beneath the water. According to local lore, it is the village of Brampton, drowned in a great storm after its inhabitants refused hospitality to a weary traveller. However, divers have found little to support the tale.

The small parking area after the main climb has a couple of benches well placed to enjoy the view. This extends out over the lowlands that run west to the city of Carlisle, with the Solway Firth beyond. All along the northern skyline, are the rolling hills of the Scottish Borders. Looking back over your left shoulder there's also a fine view of the Lakeland hills, with Helvellyn, Blencathra and Skiddaw all in the frame. A pebble mosaic representing the view over Talkin Tarn sits prettily in the foreground.

the ride

1 From the **car park** roll back down the access lane to the road and turn left, up past the **golf club** entrance, then fork left, signed to Talkin. The surroundings soon open out, with views to the **Pennines** ahead and **Talkin Tarn** down on the left. Follow the lane past **Tarn End House Hotel**, beside more golf course, then descend into

Above: Looking across fields to Talkin Tarn and the Scottish hills beyond

The level crossing at Bramptonfell Gates

1h00 **6.75 MILES** **10.9 KM** **LEVEL 2**

a small valley and climb out the other side, with one fairly steep section, into **Talkin village**. Pass the **Hare and Hounds** pub on the right to reach a junction, with the **Blacksmiths Arms** ahead.

2 Turn left on a road that's level, then descend slightly to a junction. Go right, signed to Hallbankgate. The lane climbs steadily, with a short steep section just past the rhyming **Hullerbank** and **Ullerbank**. The reward for this effort is the great view that opens up as the road levels out. The best place to enjoy this is just after another road comes in from the right, where there's a small parking area – but beware of the loose gravel.

3 Continue along the lane, enjoying level progress, with more chances to enjoy the panorama, and also the view up to the rolling moorland slopes on the right. Keep straight on past another road joining from the left; the road still runs more or less level, with only minor undulations, for about 1 mile (1.6km).

4 Not too far into the descent make a sharp left turn at **Cleugh Head**, past a pretty row of cottages and then into a fairly steep, twisting descent through shady woods. The woods open out into farmland and the gradient eases before **Kirkhouse**. Keep left here at a junction with a triangle of grass. In a little over 0.5 mile (800m), the lane runs beside **plantations** on the right.

5 Look for a rough lane, appearing more of a track, with grass down the middle, bearing off to the right just before a slight rise. This is completely unsigned but it is

MAP: OS Explorer 315 Carlisle

START/FINISH: car park at Talkin Tarn Country Park; grid ref: NY 544591

TRAILS/TRACKS: lanes, one short, slightly rougher section

LANDSCAPE: wooded farmland rising to fringes of high moorland

PUBLIC TOILETS: behind the tea room at Talkin Tarn

TOURIST INFORMATION: Brampton, tel 016977 3433

CYCLE HIRE: Scotby Cycles, Carlisle, tel 01228 546931

THE PUB: Blacksmiths Arms, Talkin Village, see Point **2** on route

🛑 The ups and down are not severe and there's a short section of rough lane. Suitability: children 7+

Getting to the start

Talkin Tarn Country Park lies 2 miles (3.2km) south east of Brampton. It is signposted from the B6413, on a lane just south of a level crossing, with a car park and tea room.

Why do this cycle ride?

From Talkin Tarn this route climbs steadily through Talkin village and on to the edge of high moors which are almost the last gasp of the Pennines. A level promenade along the heights gives huge views on a clear day. This is followed by an enjoyable descent, more pleasant lanes and an old-style level crossing just before the finish.

Researched and written by: Jon Sparks

CYCLE

Talkin Tarn CUMBRIA

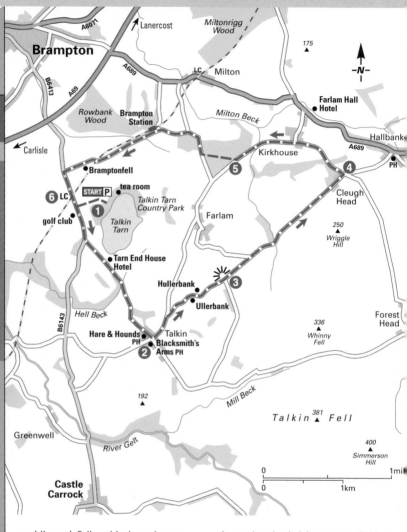

a public road. Follow this down, bumpy but with no real difficulties, until at the end it drops more steeply to a T-junction back on to real tarmac. Turn right and descend a bit more, then go up and round a bend to another junction. Go left, signed to Brampton Junction. Continue down a bit further, past a small pool in the trees on the left, to reach **Brampton Station**. Continue beside the railway. The lane eventually pulls away and rises slightly,

then swings back right to cross a bridge over the line. Keep on past the large farm of **Bramptonfell** to a T-junction and back on to the **B6413**. Turn left, and in 300yds (274m) reach the level crossing at **Bramptonfell Gates**.

6 If the gates are open, cross and continue up the road another 200yds (183m), and turn left back onto the access lane to **Talkin Tarn** and the **car park**.

Blacksmiths Arms

The 18th-century Blacksmiths Arms was originally the local smithy. Today it is all you would expect of a traditional inn: whitewashed walls without, and low-beamed ceilings, horse-brasses, plain wooden tables and local Jennings beer within the rambling small bars. Add a genuinely friendly welcome, clean and comfortable bedrooms and good value home-cooked food and you have a super base from which to explore Hadrian's Wall, the Scottish Borders and the Lake District. There's also a sheltered garden to the rear, plus a few tables at the front overlooking the village green.

Food

The well-balanced menu and blackboard specials offer a good variety of dishes, including lunchtime snacks and traditional Sunday roasts. Using meats and vegetables supplied by local farms, options include sweet-and-sour chicken, Cumberland sausage, beef lasagne, fresh haddock fillet, a vegetarian bake, venison casserole, and duck breast in orange sauce.

Family facilities

Children are welcome inside, and younger family members have their own menu to choose from.

Alternative refreshment stops

Tea room at Talkin Tarn Country Park, the Hare and Hounds in Talkin village, pubs and cafés in nearby Brampton.

about the pub

Blacksmiths Arms
Talkin Village, Brampton
Cumbria CA8 1LE
Tel 016977 3452
www.blacksmithsarmstalkin.co.uk

DIRECTIONS: on the south side of the main junction in the village
PARKING: 6 (use village lane)
OPEN: daily
FOOD: daily
BREWERY/COMPANY: free house
REAL ALE: Black Sheep Best, Jennings Cumberland Ale, guest beer
ROOMS: 5 en suite

☞ Where to go from here

Lanercost Priory is an atmospheric 12th-century ruined abbey, north east of Brampton and close to Hadrian's Wall (www.lanercost.co.uk).

Castle Carrock lime kilns

34

WALK

Through a once-industrial landscape, now peaceful and green.

Castle Carrock

CUMBRIA

Castle Carrock

The landscape around Castle Carrock has undergone many changes. Perhaps the most obvious is the reservoir, seen from above in the middle stages and at closer quarters near the end of the walk. This was completed in 1906 to provide water for the growing city of Carlisle. An army of workers was employed in the excavation and construction, and a quarry on the hillside provided stone for the dam. The local population increased by a factor of five during this period and no fewer than 12 pubs were apparently needed to quench the workers' thirsts. As you follow the route higher up the hills, the route passes the overgrown remains of several quarries.

It is perhaps less obvious that coal was also mined on these hillsides. But the most obvious sign of industrial activity is the succession of lime kilns straggling along the hillside, all at a similar level. Lime (calcium oxide) has long been valuable both as a major component of mortar (the Romans used lime mortar in Hadrian's Wall) and as a soil improver. Lime was produced by burning limestone (which is basically calcium carbonate). Originally the crushed limestone was mixed with wood, later with coal.

The lime kilns on this walk are in varying states of repair but common design features can be seen in all of them. Lime kilns were almost always built into a steep slope, allowing horses to bring the stone and fuel to the top of the kiln, from which the raw ingredients were fed in. The finest example

is seen between Points 3 and 4, where the walk crosses Totter Gill. This is an unusual double kiln in a good state of preservation.

the walk

1 Continue down past the **church** and then turn right past the **school**, on to a footpath signposted 'Garth Head'. Cross a bridge into a field, ascend left of a hedge and where it ends maintain direction through some trees. Bear slightly left on rising ground to a gate. Go up the small rise beyond, then keep the hedge on your right, up to a stile almost hidden behind a bush.

2 Bear slightly left up the bank, then cross the field to a gate in the top corner. Follow the track up through **Garth Marr** farmyard. It swings right and then continues straight on up, past **Garth Head** farmyard, and out to a lane.

3 Go left for 20yds (18m), then turn right (signposted '**Brackenthwaite**'). Follow the track ahead to a stile and continue on a more defined track, over a rise to a sudden view of the Lakeland fells. Keep following the wall down into the corner and go left through a gateway. Follow a vague track uphill, with a **wall** now on your right. Keep following this

2h00	4.5 MILES	7.2 KM	LEVEL 2

MAP: OS Explorer 315 Carlisle
START/FINISH: on street between parish church and Watson Institute, Castle Carrock; grid ref: NY 543553
PATHS: field paths, farm tracks, metalled lanes, 7 stiles
LANDSCAPE: fields, moorland with extensive views, waterside and woodland
PUBLIC TOILETS: the nearest are at Talkin Tarn
TOURIST INFORMATION: Brampton, tel 016977 3433
THE PUB: Weary Sportsman, Castle Carrock
🚸 Suitability: children 7+

Getting to the start

Castle Carrock is a small village on the B6413, about 4 miles (6.4km) south of Brampton. Go to the top of the main street, by the Weary Sportsman pub, then off the main road, and shortly left into a narrow road which runs down past the church. Park here.

Researched and written by:
Chris Bagshaw, Jon Sparks

wall to the crest of a rise, then descend a more obvious track ahead. Cross a small stream (**Totter Gill**), with a fine double lime kiln up on the left, and continue along the hillside above the wall until the track skirts a fenced-off bog. Cross a stile just beyond, go ahead to reach drier ground, then bear right and down to find a **fingerpost**.

4 Turn left and up to an obvious gate. Turn right along a narrow path above the **fence** (beware – the fence may be electrified). Pass another lime kiln on the left. Soon the path has to skirt a boggy area: keep to the base of the steeper slope for the best footing. Cross a beck and pass another lime kiln. Continue in the same vein, following a fence and then a wall on the right. Cross the wall at a stile but keep alongside it until the track bears right to pass directly in front of another **lime kiln** with trees growing out of it.

5 Follow the track down, through a gap in a wall, and then pass just left of a low tin-roofed structure – note the oven door, which suggests this is the remains

Above: Looking towards the Lake District from above Tottergill
Right: The view above Brackenthwaite with a lime kiln to the left

of a furnace. Continue down a walled track to a tarmac lane by the large farm of **Brackenthwaite**. Turn right, and go through several gates to a detached **barn**. Go right again, through a gate and up the field for 20yds (18m) to a **waymark** and boulder. Turn left and then follow a straight course through successive gates to a tarmac lane, just past a green shed.

6 Turn left. Follow the lane for 0.5 mile (800m) to an obvious track on the right, signed 'Tottergill'. Go a few paces further to a footpath sign and go right, soon joining the surfaced track alongside the **reservoir**.

what to look for

Half-way along the reservoir, the surfaced track swings away to Tottergill. Look up towards the farm and you should see an exceptionally large oak tree. Known as the Champion Oak of Cumbria, its girth has been measured at 24 feet 9 inches (approximately 7.5m). Its age is less certain but may be as much as 800 years.

Half-way along, it becomes grassy. Pass the dam and continue through woods to a road. Turn left, back into Castle Carrock.

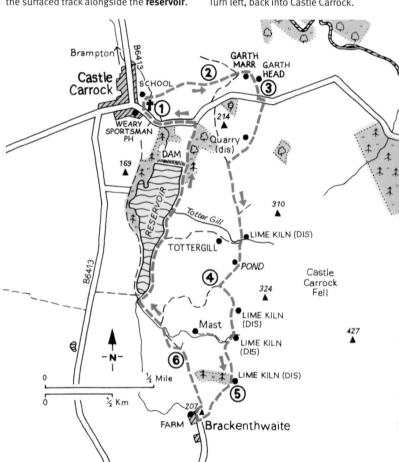

Weary Sportsman

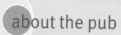

about the pub

Weary Sportsman
Castle Carrock, Brampton
Cumbria CA8 9LU
Tel 01228 670230
www.theweary.com

DIRECTIONS:	in the centre of the village
PARKING:	4
OPEN:	daily, closed Monday lunchtime
FOOD:	daily
BREWERY/COMPANY:	free house
REAL ALE:	bottled Jennings Cumberland Ale and Sneck Lifter only
DOGS:	welcome in the garden only
ROOMS:	5 en suite

From the outside the Weary Sportsman looks like a typical Cumbrian village pub. But step inside and you're in for a big surprise. If you read the sign carefully you might get a clue, as it says 'Bar and Brasserie with Rooms', but you're still likely to be surprised by the striking contemporary décor that greets you. It's what you might expect in a converted warehouse in Leeds or Manchester, not an out-of-the-way Cumbrian village. But clearly people do go out of their way to come here. The main attraction is the menu, which is as contemporary and stylish as the surroundings. Beer lovers will be disappointed that there is no real ale, although you can get Jennings Cumberland Ale or Sneck Lifter in bottled form, and traditional pub enthusiasts will still find original beams in the bar. Walkers and families are made very welcome, and there's a small sheltered patio for summer eating and drinking.

Food
The wide-ranging menu offers a cosmopolitan choice, taking in light snacks (sandwiches, baguettes and salads) and more imaginative dishes like lamb fillet (cooked to order) with wild mushroom charlotte, grape chutney and red wine jus, pheasant breast on lemon and thyme potato rosti with pepper sauce, or wild mushroom stroganoff.

Family facilities
There is no problem with children venturing into the bar. Although there is no special children's menu, small portions are available from the main menu.

Alternative refreshment stops
In Brampton, the Abbey Bridge Inn welcomes walkers, both it and the Blacksmiths Arms welcome children.

☛ Where to go from here
Take a short walk through Gelt Woods, south west of Brampton, where ancient woodland has survived in a rocky gorge above the Gelt ('mad') river. The woodland is part of an RSPB nature reserve and also the home of the Written Rock of Gelt, a vertical sandstone face bearing an inscription believed to have been carved by a Roman legionary in the 3rd century AD.

Great Asby Scar around Orton

WALK

Orton

CUMBRIA

Across some of the best limestone scenery in Cumbria.

Limestone pavements

A broken ring of limestone almost surrounds the mostly volcanic rocks of the central Lake District. On this walk it demands to be noticed, spreading out all around in great expanses of bare, fissured rock, known as limestone pavement.

Limestone is mostly composed of the bones and shells of creatures that lived in warm, shallow seas. These sometimes form obvious visible fossils, but often the remains are too small or fragmented for this to be possible. Limestone is also unusual among rocks in being soluble by water, which slowly enlarges pre-existing cracks and weaknesses. It is even more susceptible when the water is acidified by passing first through soil, and limestone pavements are normally formed under soil cover, becoming exposed only when the soil cover is lost through climate change or human intervention. Limestone pavements take many thousands of years to form, but large areas have been lost, plundered for garden rockery stone.

At first glance a limestone pavement may look bare and lifeless, but the cracks (known locally as grikes) provide shelter and home for a remarkable variety of plants. At Great Asby Scar, notable species include wood anemone, solomon's seal and bloody cranesbill, as well as ferns such as the strap-like hart's tongue. Look too for a range of moorland birds, and – on the pastures in the middle part of the walk – for hares.

In contrast to peering into the grikes, the high points on the walk also provide expansive views: east to the Pennines, with the great scoop of High Cup obvious, south to the Howgills and west to the Shap Fells on the edge of the Lake District.

the walk

1 Go straight up **Knott Lane** and through a gate at the end. Zig-zag up, steeply at first, then follow the track, with the wall just to its left, up past a small covered **reservoir**. The track becomes greener as it continues along the hillside, a little higher above the wall but still generally parallel to it, then runs almost level just above a line of low limestone scars. Gradually bear left and up slightly to a gate in a wall ahead.

Above: Herb-robert growing at Orton
Below left: Limestone scar above Orton

2 Go right. There's no clear path but aim for the lowest point of the skyline, across a grassy saddle between limestone scars. Descend slightly and go through a gate into the **Great Asby Scar Nature Reserve**. In 300yds (274m) bear right on a waymarked path. Follow this gently downhill to leave the reserve by another gate. Follow the path in the same general direction to a gate, then down a green track and its walled continuation to **Sayle Lane**.

3 Keep straight ahead for 0.25 mile (400m). Turn right on a bridleway signposted 'Sunbiggin'. Follow this track for 0.5 mile (800m), until it starts to descend.

4 Turn right, again signed 'Sunbiggin', to a gate. Go steadily uphill, keeping the wall on your left, until you drop slightly to a gate that leads to open fellside. Follow the fence on your right, cross through it at a **waymarked gate** and continue on its other side, through another gate. Keep the fence on your left to reach a gate in a wall cutting across. Look for a **marker-post** on the open ground beyond, steering you to a slot cutting through the limestone scar. Descend steadily and cross several fields towards **Sunbiggin Farm**. Skirt above the farm and follow a walled, somewhat overgrown track, out to a lane.

5 Bear right along the lane. Just past a house, turn right at a bridleway sign. Follow the path in a nearly straight line across a series of fields, eventually reaching a walled track. This is **Knott Lane** again. Turn left to return to the starting point.

3h30 — **7 MILES** — **11.3 KM** — **LEVEL 1 2 3**

WALK

MAP: OS Explorer OL19 Howgill Fells & Upper Eden Valley

START/FINISH: roadside parking near Knott Lane, 0.75 mile (1.2km) east of Orton; grid ref: NY 639079

PATHS: field paths, tracks and minor lanes, 7 stiles

LANDSCAPE: high pasture, rough grazing, limestone scars and far-reaching views

PUBLIC TOILETS: none on route

TOURIST INFORMATION: Kendal, tel 01539 725758

THE PUB: George Hotel, Orton, near the start of the route

🛈 Navigation could be tricky on open moor in poor visibility. Suitability: children 10+

Getting to the start

Orton lies north of the M6, junction 38, on the B6260. At Orton turn on to the B6261. Where this bends right keep straight ahead towards Raisbeck. In 0.75 mile (1.2km) a stony track (Knott Lane) goes off left. Park on the roadside verges or at the start of Knott Lane itself.

Researched and written by:
Chris Bagshaw, Jon Sparks

Orton

CUMBRIA

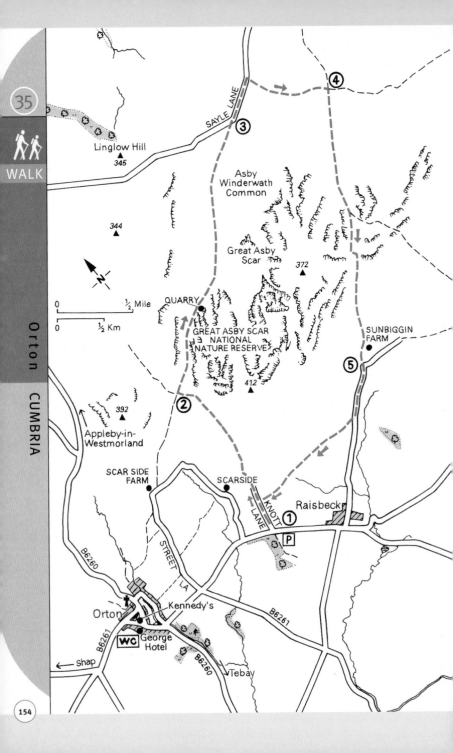

Linglow Hill
▲
345

344
▲

Asby
Winderwath
Common

Great Asby
Scar

372
▲

SAYLE LANE

③

④

0 ───── ½ Mile
0 ───── ½ Km

N

QUARRY ●

GREAT ASBY SCAR
NATIONAL
NATURE RESERVE

412
▲

SUNBIGGIN
FARM ●

⑤

392
▲

②

Appleby-in-
Westmorland

SCAR SIDE
FARM ●

SCARSIDE ●

Raisbeck

KNOTT LANE

①

P

STREET LA

B6260

B6261

Orton

Kennedy's

WC George
Hotel

← Shap

B6261

B6260

Tebay

B6261

George Hotel

Food

A blackboard menu changes regularly and highlights dishes prepared from fresh local and seasonal produce. In addition to lighter snacks like sandwiches and ploughman's lunches, you'll find Angus steaks, fresh fish dishes, home-cooked gammon and home-made curries, perhaps lamb balti.

Family facilities

Children are welcome in the bars and overnight, and there's a children's menu.

☛ Where to go from here

North west of Orton, visit the remains of Shap Abbey (open access), which is set in prime walking country on the banks of the River Lowther.

The George sits solidly at the centre of Orton village and is equally at the centre of village life. Locals and visitors are both made welcome and, with the pub on the Coast to Coast Walk route, walkers are very much catered for. There's a cosy lounge bar with log fire and a non-smoking dining room. The lower bar, known as the taproom, is the place to go if you have muddy boots. If the weather is good, there is plenty of garden space, on three levels, to relax in with a drink. There's a choice of real ales, with Greene King IPA and one or two guest beers from local breweries on handpump.

about the pub

George Hotel
Front Street, Orton
Penrith, Cumbria CA10 3RJ
Tel 01539 624229
www.georgehotel.net

DIRECTIONS: in the centre of Orton village
PARKING: no car park; plenty of roadside parking
OPEN: daily, all day summer
FOOD: closed Monday lunchtime in winter
BREWERY/COMPANY: free house
REAL ALE: Green King IPA, guest beers
DOGS: well-behaved dogs are welcome inside
ROOMS: 7 en suite

Kirkby Lonsdale to Whittington

From the old market town to Whittington village, on the Cumbria/Lancashire border.

The Lune Valley

It's something of a revelation to escape the weekend motorcycle congregation on Devil's Bridge and take this circular walk over rolling hills, through farmland and woods, to the worthy village of Whittington, then to return along the banks of the lovely Lune. You pass close to Sellet Mill: its huge waterwheel, incorporated within the building, was reputedly once the second largest in the country. Corn was ground at the mill until its closure in the 1940s. Sellet is an old local word for a drumlin – a small rounded hill formed by glacial deposits. Your next Sellet is Sellet Bank, which appears to be a large drumlin. The walk takes you around its base and eventually to Sellet Hall. Built as a farm in 1570 by the Baines family, the hall was possibly once used as a hospital, as it is situated at the end of Hosticle Lane – 'hosticle' is an old dialect word for hospital.

A spring in a field at Newbiggin-on-Lune is the source of the beautiful River Lune, which eventually flows into Morecambe Bay and the Irish Sea, north of Cockersand Abbey. The river has inspired many artists, most famously J M W Turner, who visited Kirkby Lonsdale in 1818 and subsequently included the river in two of his paintings. The riverbed is rocky under the graceful 14th-century Devil's Bridge, so called because it was supposedly provided by the Devil to enable a poor widow to reach her cow on the opposite bank.

In return for this the Devil was to acquire the soul of the first being to cross the bridge. The widow's only other possession was a small dog. According to a popular poem from the 1820s, she threw a bun across the bridge and the poor hound scampered after it, thus thwarting the Devil and saving her own soul.

the walk

1 From the west bank of the river, a few paces downstream from **Devil's Bridge**, go diagonally up across a park with picnic tables to a kissing gate onto the **A65**. Cross over, go through a narrow meadow and between houses to cross the **B6254**. As you enter another meadow, go uphill, keeping the walled wooded area on your left. Keep on over the brow of the hill and straight ahead through two stiles. Turn left at another gap stile into the farmyard at **Wood End Farm**.

2 Turn right on the farm track towards white-painted **Wood End Cottage**. Go left in front of the cottage along a sometimes overgrown walled path, which is remarkably rough in places. A stream comes in from the left and tries to take over the path, but drier ground is just around the corner. The path opens out by **Sellet Mill's millpond**, with good views of Ingleborough over the water.

The Devil's Bridge across the River Lune in Kirkby Lonsdale dates from the 15th century

2h30 · 4.75 MILES · 7.7 KM · LEVEL 1 2 3

3 Turn right by the cluster of **farm buildings** and walk up the field, keeping the fence to your left, until just past the end of a garden. Go left through a **yellow marked gate** and walk straight across a small field to another marked gate, followed immediately by a shallow stream. Bear right to skirt round a rounded hill (**Sellet Bank**), aiming initially for the corner of a hedge under a row of pylons. Continue with the hedge to your right, taking time to look back at good views of Leck Fell and Barbon Fell.

4 Go through a yellow marked stile on your right, then skirt round a wooded area to reach **Sellet Hall**. Turn right and follow the wooden fence, with marker arrows, then keep on over the corner of the field to cross a stile and drop down a couple of steps to the road at a T-junction. Turn left along a lane (**Hosticle Lane**) towards Whittington village.

5 The tall trees of **Hagg Wood** are on your right and hazel and hawthorn hedges are beside you as you follow the lane down to **Whittington**.

6 Go left at the T-junction for a few paces, then cross the road and turn right over a pebbled mosaic to the **Church of St Michael the Archangel**. Keep the square bell tower on your left before descending stone steps to go through a narrow stile and the modern graveyard. Proceed through a gate in the left corner and keep straight ahead across two small fields to a stone stile leading to a narrow, walled lane. Emerging onto **Main Street**, turn right, in front of a lovely building dated 1875, and follow the road past the **village hall** and the **Dragon's Head** pub.

MAP: OS Explorer OL2 Yorkshire Dales – Southern & Western

START/FINISH: Devil's Bridge car park, Kirkby Lonsdale; grid ref: SD 615782

PATHS: a little overgrown and indistinct in patches, quiet lanes and tracks, plenty of stiles

LANDSCAPE: rolling hills, farmland, riverbank, good distance views

PUBLIC TOILETS: at Devil's Bridge car park, and behind the pub in Whittington

TOURIST INFORMATION: Kirkby Lonsdale, tel 015242 71437

THE PUB: Dragon's Head, Whittington, see Point **7** on route

🅛 Very rough path after Wood End Farm. Suitability: children 6+

Getting to the start

Kirkby Lonsdale is a market town just off the A65. Turn north off the A65 on the A683, cross the bridge, and then take the next, sharp, right turn to the car park above Devil's Bridge.

Researched and written by: Sheila Bowker, Jon Sparks

Vicarage beyond St Mary's churchyard in Kirkby Londsdale

Kirkby Lonsdale

CUMBRIA/LANCASHIRE

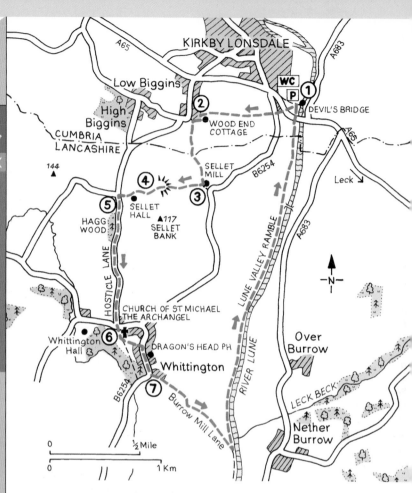

7 At a sharp right bend on the edge of the village turn left along a gritty track, passing a farm and tennis court. Follow the track as it winds its way between fields to reach a pair of gates. Go through the left-hand gate (cattle grid). Bear left to pick up the riverside walk – the **Lune Valley Ramble**. This is overgrown at the start but soon becomes an easy walk through fields. Follow it back to the **A65 bridge** at **Kirkby Lonsdale**. Go through a gate and up steps to the left of the parapet. Cross the road, and drop down the other side to cross the park at the start of the walk.

what to look for

When you walk down the track after Whittington, you'll pass what looks like a steeplechase fence – and that's almost exactly what it is. Whittington still hosts regular Point-to-Point races, harking back to one of the earliest forms of horse racing. You can see several more fences in the same line.

Dragon's Head

*How often can you post a letter inside
a pub? At the Dragon's Head you can.
On Tuesdays and Thursdays the publican
turns postmaster as the village post
office is actually housed within the pub.
This sort of doubling-up is common
enough in rural Ireland and becoming
more so in parts of Scotland too, but is
still very rare in England. It's just one of
the ways in which the Dragon's Head
stands out. On a more conventional level,
this homely village local is notable for
many original features, especially the
fine panelled and mirrored bar. It also
has a boules pitch and its own caravan
site out at the back – with a fine view of
the Lune Valley and the unmistakable
outline of Ingleborough.*

Food

In keeping with the unspoilt charm and
atmosphere of the pub, food is simple
and home-made and may include braised
steak, steak pie, cod and chips and
gammon and chips.

about the pub

Dragon's Head
Main Street, Whittington
Carnforth, Lancashire LA6 2NY
Tel 015242 72383

DIRECTIONS: near the centre of the village,
south east of the church
PARKING: 10
OPEN: daily, closed Monday lunchtime
FOOD: daily
BREWERY/COMPANY: Mitchells
REAL ALE: Tetley, Lancaster Bomber,
guest beers
DOGS: welcome inside

Family facilities

Children are welcome in the games room.
On fine days they can amuse themselves
in the garden and, perhaps, take on the
grown-ups at a game of boules.

Alternative refreshment stops

There are usually a couple of vans at
Devil's Bridge, one selling ices and the
other drinks and snacks.

☛ Where to go from here

Visit Kirkby Lonsdale, which has a market
charter from the 13th century, and still hosts
a market every Thursday around the unusual
20th-century butter cross. There are some
fine 17th- and 18th-century buildings, and
famous views from the churchyard.

From Sedbergh to Brigflatts

A gentle walk from the historic town to a Quaker hamlet.

Sedbergh

The solid, stone-built town of Sedbergh is one of the largest settlements in the Yorkshire Dales National Park. It is dominated by two things: the Howgill Fells, especially the southernmost peaks of Winder and Crook, and the famous Sedbergh School, which wraps itself around much of the town's south side.

The area is noted for its Quaker associations. In 1652 the founder of the Society of Friends, George Fox, came to the town and preached from a bench beneath a yew tree in the churchyard to a great crowd of people attending the Hiring Fair. On Firbank Fell, north west of Sedbergh, Fox again preached to a large crowd, this time from a big stone, still known as Fox's Pulpit. This meeting is said to mark the

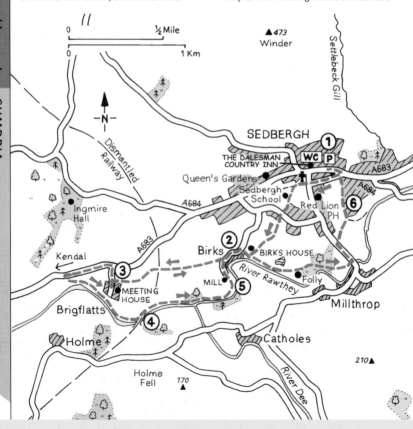

what to look for

The Howgill Fells are huge, rounded humps that seem to crowd in on each other like elephants at a watering hole. They are formed from pinkish sandstone and slates, 100 million years older than the limestone that underlies much of the rest of the area. The hills have few of the stone walls you will see elsewhere in the Dales – they are mostly common grazing land for the local farms and escaped the passion for enclosure in earlier centuries.

inception of the Society of Friends. Fox wrote, 'This was the place that I had seen a people coming forth in white raiment; and a mighty meeting there was and it is to this day near Sedbergh which I gathered in the name of Jesus.'

Fox stayed at the tiny hamlet of Brigflatts in 1652, and in 1674 the Friends of the district decided to build a Meeting House. It still survives, one of the oldest in England. From the outside it looks like a typical whitewashed cottage of the period, though, unlike most dwellings, it had a stone roof from the start.

the walk

1 From the **car park**, turn right along the main street, continue to the junction with the main road and turn left. Below the churchyard turn right, signposted 'Cattle Market or Busk Lane'. At the next signpost go left, behind the **cricket pavilion**, then straight ahead across a drive, through a kissing gate and down to a road. Cross slightly left and go through another kissing gate, signed 'Birks'. Follow the track, with more playing fields on your right, to another gate. Bear right on a green path across a field. Skirt round **Birks House** and continue to a kissing gate.

The Friends Meeting House in Brigflatts was built in 1674

 1h30 — **4.5 MILES** — **7.2 KM** — **LEVEL 1**23

MAP: OS Explorer OL19 Howgill Fells & Upper Eden Valley

START/FINISH: pay-and-display car park just off Sedbergh main street; grid ref: SD 659921

PATHS: mostly on field and riverside paths, 7 stiles

LANDSCAPE: playing fields give way to rich farmland, dominated by fells

PUBLIC TOILETS: at car park

TOURIST INFORMATION: Kendal, tel 01539 725758

THE PUB: The Dalesman Country Inn, Sedbergh, near the start of the route

🔴 A section of road-walking alongside the A683 can be avoided by shortening the walk at Point 3. Suitability: children 6+

Getting to the start

Sedburgh is at the junction of the A683 and the A684, east of Kendal. Approaching from the west, keep straight ahead through the town and along the narrow cobbled main street to find the car park on the left. Note, the main street is one-way, running west-to-east.

Researched and written by:
Jon Sparks, David Winpenny

Sedbergh

CUMBRIA

The confluence of the rivers Rawthey and Dee near Sedbergh

2 Go through the kissing gate and turn left along the lane through the cluster of houses at **Birks**. Opposite the entrance to the **Old Barn** go through a kissing gate and bear half left (the Brigflatts sign points too far left) to a **waymarker**. Continue, keeping the wall on your left, in an almost straight line, to a small bridge taking you under the old railway. Drop down and bear slightly left on a path across the fields to a gate, which leads on to a quiet lane opposite the **Quaker burial ground**.

3 Turn left to visit the **Meeting House**, then return to the gate. (Note, beyond here is some walking along a main road with poor verges. To avoid this, retrace your steps to **Birks** – but you'll miss out on some of the best riverside walking.) To continue, walk up the lane to the main road and turn left. Just beyond a bend sign on the left is a lay-by where you'll find a signposted metal kissing gate in the hedge. Follow the narrow path, elevated above the **River Rawthey**, then drop down to riverbank level, to a large railway bridge.

4 Go through the gate and diagonally up the side of the embankment.

Cross and go straight back down to the river. Continue along the riverside, passing the confluence of the Rawthey and the Dee, and reach a tarmac lane by an **old mill**.

5 Follow the lane back into **Birks**. Go right, though the kissing gate signposted 'Rawthey Way' (you went through this gate the other way earlier in the walk). By the hedge around **Birks House**, bear right and down towards the river. Follow the river, beside another playing field, to a stile. Climb slightly left to a gap in a wall and continue past a **folly**. Walk along the left side of a wood, then enter it at a kissing gate. Bear right at a footpath sign and join an unusual sunken path. Leave the wood, cross a stile and follow a clear path across a field to emerge onto a road by a bridge. Turn left. By the 'Welcome to Sedbergh' **sign**, go right, though a stile. Cross the field to another stile, then bear left beside a large grey building to another kissing gate.

6 Cross a drive, go downhill and straight on to the main road. Cross the road then turn left at the 'No Entry' sign, along Sedbergh's main street to the **car park** or continue to **The Dalesman Country Inn**.

The Dalesman Country Inn

Walk out the front door of this village inn, take a couple of right turns and within five minutes you can be raising your pulse rate on the steep slopes of Winder, southernmost of the Howgill Fells, or strolling alongside the River Dee. Inside, the 16th-century former coaching inn has been modernised without losing its character, and the pub is renowned for its amazing floral displays. Expect stripped stone and beams, a mix of farmhouse chairs around copper-topped tables, log-effect gas fires, and top-notch Black Sheep Bitter on handpump. The bonus of comfortable accommodation makes this a popular stop with walkers tackling the Dales Way.

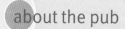

about the pub

The Dalesman Country Inn
Sedbergh
Cumbria LA10 5BN
Tel 015396 21183
www.thedalesman.co.uk

DIRECTIONS: on the main street west of the car park	
PARKING: 8	
OPEN: daily, all day	
FOOD: daily	
BREWERY/COMPANY: free house	
REAL ALE: Theakston Best Bitter, Black Sheep Bitter, guest ale	
DOGS: welcome in the bar	
ROOMS: 7 en suite	

Food
The lunchtime menu concentrates on straightforward, nourishing fare – club sandwiches, home-made soups and pies. The evening offerings can be considerably more imaginative, perhaps noisettes of lamb with roast plums and basil mash.

Family facilities
Families with young children are very welcome inside the bars. Kids have their own menu, and there's outdoor patio seating and a garden.

Alternative refreshment stops
The Bull in Sedbergh also offers meals at lunchtime and evenings, while the Red Lion has lunches (not Mondays). There are two cafés in the town, too. Locals recommend the Post Horn, opposite the church.

☛ Where to go from here
One of the spectacular sights of the Dales, the great ribbon of waterfalls known as Cautley Spout is worth the drive north from Sedbergh, in the direction of Kirkby Stephen. Park by the Cross Keys, a temperance inn. You can view the falls from there or walk part of the way towards it on a good path.

From Dent along the Dales Way

Dent CUMBRIA

From the birthplace of a geologist, through the countryside that inspired him.

The village of Dent

Sometimes called 'the hidden valley', Dentdale is unlike most of the Yorkshire Dales as it looks west towards the Lake District, and at its western end the lime-stone landscape gives way to the rounded Howgill Fells. Its 'capital', Dent, is highly individual, with its dog-legged main street lined with stone cottages that front directly on to the cobbles, or cluster around the church. In the main street, a drinking-fountain made from a huge boulder of Shap granite is inscribed 'Adam Sedgwick 1785–1873'. It is a bold and simple memorial to Dent's most famous son.

Born in the Old Parsonage by the village green, Sedgwick studied at Sedbergh School before going on to Cambridge University, where his study of geology, inspired by the rocks of Dentdale, made him a leading authority. He eventually became Professor of Geology at Cambridge, and the university's geology museum is named after him. Sedgwick returned regularly to Dent. 'Whenever I have revisited the hills and dales of my native country,' he wrote in 1866, 'I have felt a new swell of emotion, and said to myself, here is the land of my birth; this was the home of my boyhood, and is still the home of my heart.'

the walk

1 Leave the **car park**, turn left, then right beside the **Memorial Hall**. Pass the **green** and the **Sun Inn** and keep straight on at the 'Flinter Gill' signpost. The tarmac lane becomes a steep stony track climbing through trees beside **Flinter Gill**. Slowly the gradient eases and the trees peter out. Finally you reach a wooden gate beside a **seat**, high on the fellside. Go through the gate to a T-junction of tracks.

Whitewashed stone cottages and the memorial to Adam Sedgwick in Dent village

WALK

2 Turn right, signed 'Keldishaw'. Follow the walled track for 1.5 miles (2.4km), keeping straight ahead at the only junction. The track is heavily rutted in places due to its illicit use by motor vehicles, but the walking is always easy. Eventually the track reaches a tarmac road. Turn right for 0.25 mile (400m) to the crest of a rise and **signpost** to Underwood on the left.

3 Go through the gate and follow the grassy track past small shake-holes to a **ladder stile**. Continue along a dilapidated wall to reach a track. This bears right below a slope scattered with trees, then contours round with great views of the valley, eventually descending through the yard of a **ruined farmhouse**.

4 Go round the ruined house; its back windows look straight down a green track. Follow this, winding down the hill, crossing a couple of tumbledown walls before **marker posts**, below and left, steer you away from the track. Drop down to the **stream**, go left along the bank for a few paces, then cross a simple bridge of two stones. Climb the bank beyond and go straight ahead through the **farmyard**.

5 Continue down the farm track until it almost levels out beside a line of trees. Turn left by a large oak and go through a waymarked gate. Walk diagonally across the field towards another **ruined farmhouse** with elder trees growing all over it. Pass just to its right and continue down, soon picking up a clearer track. Follow this downhill to reach a drive and go right a few paces to a **tarmac lane**.

MAP: OS Explorer OL2 Yorkshire Dales – Southern & Western

START/FINISH: pay-and-display car park, west end of Dent; grid ref: SD 704871

PATHS: tracks, field and riverside paths, some roads, 13 stiles

LANDSCAPE: moorland and farmland, with wide views of Dentdale

PUBLIC TOILETS: at car park

TOURIST INFORMATION: Kendal, tel 01539 725758

THE PUB: Sun Inn, Dent, near start of route

🚶 Suitability: children 6+

Getting to the start

Dent village lies about 6 miles (9.6km) south east of Sedbergh. Go through Sedbergh on the A684, turn right just before the narrow cobbled section of the main street and follow the road into Dentdale. The car park is on the left as you approach the old heart of the village.

Researched and written by:
Jon Sparks, David Winpenny

Dent   CUMBRIA

6 Turn left along the lane. Follow it round to the right and then back left as it levels out in the valley bottom. Look for a ladder stile by a barn on the left. Don't use this, but look out for a **signpost**, about 50 paces further on the right, with a plank bridge and stile just below it. From the stile follow the path across the field to the riverbank. Go right, following the river (and the **Dales Way**) upstream for about 0.75 mile (1.2km) to reach stone steps leading to a squeeze stile and onto a stone bridge.

7 Go straight across the road and down more steps to continue along the riverside path, until it finally joins the road. Turn left along the road (take care as there are no real verges at first) and follow it back in to **Dent**.

what to look for

As you climb up steeply by Flinter Gill, you'll pass a gate beside a barn. About 50 paces above this, take a short detour to the left on a level path to where the stream tumbles over some rock steps after rain. A little higher up there may be water in the gill, even if it's not pouring out over the rocks below. This is typical of limestone country, where the water often disappears down fissures in the soluble rock. Higher up, look for 'bomb craters' in the moorland. Known as shake-holes, these too are typical of limestone country, and are due to the action of water finding its way down weaknesses in the rock. Over time these may enlarge to become open shafts.

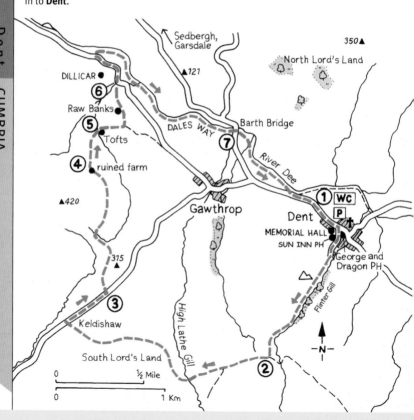

Sun Inn

about the pub

Sun Inn
Main Street, Dent
Sedbergh, Cumbria LA10 5QL
Tel 015396 25208

DIRECTIONS: centre of the village, close by the Memorial Hall	
PARKING: 10 (use village car park)	
OPEN: daily, all day	
FOOD: daily	
BREWERY/COMPANY: Dent Brewery	
REAL ALE: Dent Bitter, Aviator, Kamikaze and T'Owd Tup	
DOGS: welcome in the bar	
ROOMS: 3 bedrooms	

Serving as a magnet for dale walkers and real ale buffs, the Sun stands at the heart of pretty Dent village, surrounded by quaint, 16th-century whitewashed cottages and narrow cobbled streets, and must be one of the most photographed pubs in Cumbria. Its cosy bars, with original coin-studded beams, open coal fire and local photographs are entirely in keeping with the setting. The pub is a family business and the same family also operate the Dent Brewery, just up the road, so the quality of the ales is guaranteed. Benches at the front and adjoining the small car park look out over the village green to the distant fells.

Food

The food is no-nonsense traditional pub grub, well prepared and in generous portions. Typically, tuck into local Cumberland sausages, home-made chicken and ham pie and braised lamb in root vegetable gravy.

Family facilities

The pub welcomes children and offers a standard children's menu.

Alternative refreshment stops

Dent's other pub, the George and Dragon, also serves excellent Dent Brewery beers and offers good food, as do the tea rooms in the village.

☛ Where to go from here

Visit the Sedgwick Geological Trail beside the A684 in neighbouring Garsdale, where you can find out more about Adam Sedgwick and his geological discoveries. To the east is the typical Dales landscape of the Yoredale series of sedimentary rocks and to the west the much older Silurian rocks of the Howgill Fells – geologically part of the Lake District.

From Garrigill to Ashgill Force

A broad valley hides exciting waterfalls and ravines.

Garrigill

As you approach the village, with the long ascent over Hartside, on one of the highest main roads in the country, you cross the main watershed of England. Below is the valley of the South Tyne, its waters feeding not west to the Irish Sea but east to the North Sea. The landscape is different from

the Lake District, the hills big, bare and simple in their outlines.

It might appear that this landscape has changed little for centuries. The truth is, of course, that few English landscapes are static, and this is no exception. Today's generally pastoral scene conceals the scars of an industrial past. Garrigill's population in the mid-19th century was five or six times what it is today. Two main trends lie behind this decline, one being that fewer people work on the land today, while the second factor

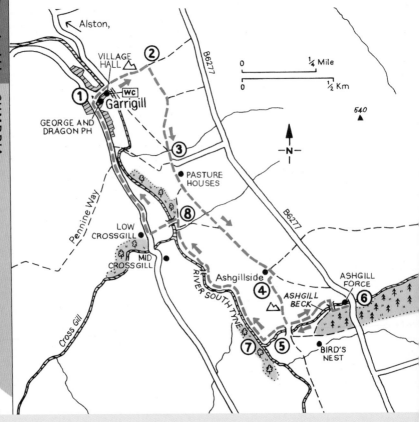

View across Garrigill and the South Tyne Valley

has been the disappearance of the once-dominant lead-mining industry. Mining developed rapidly from the mid-18th century onwards, largely under the control of the Quaker-owned London Lead Mining Company, which built houses, schools and reading rooms for its workers and their families. Garrigill was virtually a 'company town'. Sharp eyes will be able to spot traces of this industry on the upper slopes. Look out, in particular, for sharp V-shaped valleys cut into the moorland, many of which are artificial. Known as hushes, they were created by damming a stream and then allowing the water to escape in a flash flood. This was a relatively quick and easy way of stripping off the topsoil to expose the rocks beneath.

the walk

1 Walk down the road in front of the **post office** and the **George & Dragon Inn** (signposted 'Alston, Nenthead') to a bridge high above the river **South Tyne**. The road bends left but a track continues straight ahead. Follow this track, very steep at first, to reach a tarmac lane at a bend.

2 Turn right immediately, signed to **Pasture Houses**, go through a gate and straight across a field. Cross a stile and continue to a gate below some new and restored buildings, and then to a stile. Bear right, descending slightly, towards a **farm** and trees. Go through a gate in the field corner and then along the left (upper) side of the **barn**. Cross the yard diagonally to a track which leads out to a road.

1h30 — **3 MILES** — **4.8 KM** — **LEVEL 1 2 3**

MAP: OS Explorer OL31 North Pennines

START/FINISH: parking on green in front of post office, Garrigill; grid ref: NY 7444150

PATHS: field paths, tracks and a quiet lane, 17 stiles

LANDSCAPE: open fields, wooded river valley with cascades and waterfalls

PUBLIC TOILETS: beside village hall, just before bridge at start of walk

TOURIST INFORMATION: Alston Moor, tel 01434 382244

THE PUB: George & Dragon Inn, Garrigill, see Point **1** on route

❶ Path runs above steep drops to river. Suitability: children 7+

Getting to the start

Garrigill lies south east of the village of Alston, which is at the junction of the A686 and the A689, due south of Haltwhistle. From Alston take the B6277 and turn off right. In Garrigill, park considerately around the village green.

Researched and written by:
Chris Bagshaw, Jon Sparks

Garrigill   CUMBRIA

3 Cross directly to a stile. Follow the wall below gardens on the left, then continue straight ahead to a stile. Keep straight ahead and level to another stile, then aim for another **farm** ahead. Go left of the first building and into the yard, then go left and right between the houses to a stile where the lane bends left again. Cross a short field and emerge onto a track. Cross this, and the **paddock** beyond, to a stile. Turn right, along the back of a house and through a gateway into a field.

4 Turn left and follow a green track, initially parallel to the wall and then descending to a **footbridge** and four-way fingerpost.

5 Don't cross the bridge but turn left (signposted 'Ashgill Force') and follow a path left of **Ashgill Beck**. Follow this, passing some small cataracts, to a footbridge with the main falls visible ahead. Cross the bridge and continue to the **falls**, passing **old mine workings** on the right. It's possible to walk right behind the falls, but be careful as the surface is loose, and often wet and slippery too.

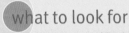

Looking from behind Ashgill Force waterfall with the river running down the valley

6 Retrace your steps, crossing the first footbridge, to the lower footbridge by the four-way **fingerpost**. Now continue downhill, still following **Ashgill Beck**.

7 Where Ashgill Beck meets the River South Tyne, cross a stile on to the riverside path (**South Tyne Trail** waymarks). Follow the path, paved with flagstones in places, above a wooded gorge-like section. Where the river curves away to the left, it's possible to continue straight ahead across a rushy field. Go past a bridge (to **Mid Crossgill**) and continue along the river, under tall pines (watch for red squirrels here), to reach another four-way fingerpost.

8 Turn left across the **bridge**; walk up the track to a gate opposite **Low Crossgill** farm. Turn right along the road into **Garrigill**.

what to look for

Ashgill Force waterfall is the most striking sight on the walk. The stream has carved itself a significant gorge. A harder band of limestone has resisted its efforts while the softer shales below have been cut back, creating an overhang which allows you to walk right behind the fall, which is approximately 50ft (15m) high. There are several smaller but still lovely cascades lower down the course of the beck before it joins the South Tyne.

George & Dragon Inn

The 17th-century George & Dragon Inn occupies a unique position, where the best-known of Britain's long-distance walks, the Pennine Way, crosses perhaps its most popular major cycle route, the C2C. Needless to say, walkers and cyclists are big business here, and the owners know exactly what their priorities are. On bleak Pennine days, getting warm and dry is often the first priority and a blazing fire in the homely, stone-flagged bar helps. There's also an attractive stone and panelled dining room and four new bedrooms. Robust appetites and hearty thirsts are well looked after, the latter with foaming pints of Black Sheep or local micro-brewery ales. The pub is also a mini information centre with maps, leaflets and advice all on hand.

Food

The menu concentrates on traditional pub favourites, done well: the Cumberland sausage is from a butcher in nearby Alston, the game pie home-made. Non-carnivores are recommended to try the vegetarian moussaka. Snacks include sandwiches, filled jacket potatoes and a giant Yorkshire pudding filled with steak and gravy.

Family facilities

Children are welcome in the lounge and dining room until 9.30pm. In summer there's alfresco seating on the village green.

☛ Where to go from here

Visit Alston, England's highest market town, 1,000 feet (305m) above sea level, with steep cobbled streets and many 17th-century buildings. It's also home to the narrow-gauge South Tynedale

about the pub

George & Dragon Inn
Garrigill, Alston
Cumbria CA9 3DS
Tel 01434 381293
www.garrigill-pub.com

39

WALK

Garrigill

CUMBRIA

DIRECTIONS: centre of Garrigill, at the start of the walk

PARKING: village green

OPEN: daily, and all day Saturday and Sunday from Easter to October. Closed Monday to Thursday lunchtime in winter

FOOD: daily

BREWERY/COMPANY: free house

REAL ALE: Black Sheep Bitter, 3 guest beers

DOGS: welcome inside

ROOMS: 4 bedrooms

Railway running on part of the route of the (standard-gauge) Haltwhistle-to-Alston branch line. A few miles away, the Nenthead Mines Heritage Centre gives a real insight into the area's lead-mining past, and you can even venture underground to see exactly what a mine was like.

A walk through Grisedale from Garsdale Head

The derelict farmsteads of this once-thriving dale on the Cumbria/North Yorkshire boundary tell their own story.

Grisedale

Grisedale pushes north from Garsdale towards the massive heights of Wild Boar Fell, and is sometimes tagged 'The Dale that Died'. This unfortunate label was the title of a television documentary made in the mid-1970s that followed the fortunes – and misfortunes – of families farming in this remote valley. The programme focused on a former miner, Joe Gibson, who struggled against the weather, ill luck and the lack of subsidies for upland farmers to try to make even a bare living from the land – a struggle that eventually proved unequal and ended with his retreat from Grisedale.

The fields that Joe and his neighbours tended have reverted to moor and scrub, and a plantation of conifers climbs the side of East Baugh Fell from the valley bottom. Nearly all the farmhouses in the upper part of the dale are now derelict. At the head of the valley stands Round Ing, once a substantial building with barns and animal sheds. Now it has tumbled down, its walls diminishing in height every year. What remains of the plants and shrubs in its garden still bloom in summer, but, like West Scale and East Scale a little downstream, it is a place of sadness and lost hope.

Grisedale's earlier history is obscure. Its name comes from Old Norse and means 'the valley in which the pigs were kept', so the dale must have been farmed from its earliest days. In the Middle Ages it was owned by the monks of Jervaulx Abbey.

the walk

1 Walk down the hill from the station to the **main road**. Cross just above the junction and take a stile signed to Grisedale and Flust. Follow a faint path a little above the wall on the left, to find another stile in a wall. Follow the sign straight ahead on a narrow path across the field to another **signpost**. This points down the field, aiming a little right of **Blake Mire** farmhouse, to another stile beyond the bend of the wall.

2 Go half right from this stile, aiming slightly left of a **barn** to find the remains of a stile in a crumbling wall. Continue straight ahead and descend to some **ruined buildings**. Pass between them and then turn right, over a stile. Follow the sign towards a barn to find another little gate/stile behind it. Now aim for a **white-painted farmhouse** and then skirt left around it to a signpost.

3 Cross the lane to another **signpost**, which points to yet another stile. Cross this and bear left along the wall, then descend to follow the beck. Go through a gate and, just before the barn at **Reachey**, bear right, up the valley, to a signposted stile. From this follow the beck upstream to a little humpback bridge near the ruins of **East Scale**. Do not cross the bridge, but follow two signposts uphill and then along the brink of the steeper slope above the stream. The ruins of **Round Ing** are the next destination, but the tall **sycamore** that stands beside them is easier to spot.

2h15 — **5 MILES** — **8 KM** — **LEVEL 2 3**

4 From Round Ing double back, following the signpost towards **East House**. There is no clear path, but keep right of the crest of the rising ground ahead, then look for a **waymarked post** by the corner of a wall. Continue towards the right-hand end of a small plantation on the hillside. As you get nearer, look for an obvious track on the right, leading to a barn below the plantation. Just before the barn, bear right, off the track, to a gate under some trees. Go through the gate and cross the stream.

5 Follow the wall on the right, pass a small ruin and continue straight across the field towards the farm at **Feafow**. Cross a wooden stile and then a ladder stile right of the **farm buildings**. Join the farm track and follow it to a metalled road. Turn left, uphill, to a T-junction, where the tarmac ends. Turn right along the track. The track becomes less clear but keep straight ahead over level moorland to a stile beside a gate. Bear slightly left, down the hill. There's no clear path but when the slope steepens aim for the **grey footbridge** over the railway, with a house alongside.

A humpback bridge over a stream near the ruins of East Scale

MAP: OS Explorer OL19 Howgill Fells & Upper Eden Valley

START/FINISH: roadside parking on road to Garsdale Station; grid ref: SD 786919

PATHS: moorland paths and tracks, may be boggy, 19 stiles

LANDSCAPE: rough moors and hidden valleys, railway within earshot

PUBLIC TOILETS: none on route

TOURIST INFORMATION: Kendal, tel 01539 725758

THE PUB: The Moorcock Inn, Garsdale Head, off route

🛈 Navigation very tricky on open moor in poor visibility. Suitability: children 9+

Getting to the start

Garsdale Head and Garsdale Station are on the A684 between Sedbergh and Hawes, 10 miles (16.1km) east of Sedbergh. There's a turning for Garsdale Station, with limited roadside parking a short way up.

Researched and written by:
Jon Sparks, David Winpenny

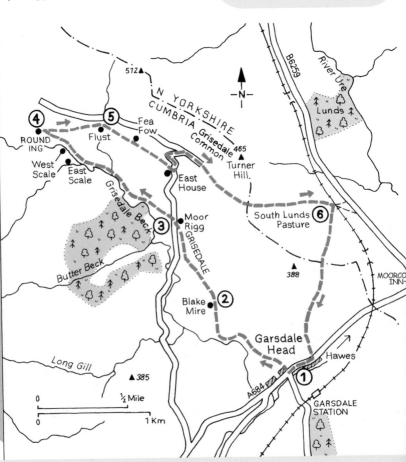

6 Go over a stile left of the house, pass the **footbridge** and then cross a stile in a corner close to the line. Walk half right, away from the railway – the path is faint but clear enough. Pass through a **tumbled wall** and bear slightly left up the steeper slope, then follow the path, bearing slightly right, over the crest to a prominent **ladder stile**. A clearer path beyond this leads across the slope and soon descends to meet the main road opposite a **line of cottages**. It's probably best to cross right away as the verge on the far side is safer. Turn right, back to the road junction and the parking place.

what to look for

Most of this walk is across rough pasture and moorland, the preferred habitat for many species of ground-nesting birds – so do watch where you're putting your feet, especially in spring and early summer. The largest of these birds is the curlew, with mottled brown plumage, a long down-curved bill and an evocative bubbling cry. Another that you can hardly miss is the lapwing. From a distance they appear black and white but close up show a green sheen on back and wings and a distinctive crest. Their alarm call gives them the alternative name 'peewit'.